UNDER ONE FLAG

How indigenous and ethnic peoples of the Commonwealth and former British Empire helped Great Britain win World War II

Erica Myers-Davis

HRH The Prince Philip
Duke of Edinburgh KG KT
Grand President
Royal Commonwealth
Ex-Services League

The Royal Commonwealth Ex-Services League was founded in 1921 by Field Marshals Earl Haig and Jan Smuts with the aim to 'ensure that no Commonwealth ex-serviceman or woman, who has at some time served the British Crown before their country achieved independence of the United Kingdom, is without help if in need'. The League continues this work by providing welfare support to thousands of Commonwealth veterans, many of whom are now old and frail.

Today there are 56 Member Organisations in 48 Countries that make up the League and the Charity acts as a link throughout the Commonwealth for many ex-service organisations and provides financial assistance for eligible beneficiaries. Additionally, financial support is also given to self help projects that will generate income for local welfare.

To find out more about our work visit www.commonwealthveterans.org.uk. Proceeds from this book will continue to support the work that the League does in helping our veterans live the remainder of the lives in peace and dignity.

First published in Great Britain in 2009 by
Get Publishing
underoneflag@hotmail.com

An imprint of Get Publishing, 1a Arcade House,
Finchley Road, London NW11 7TL
Registered Company 7011875

Text copyright © Erica Myers-Davis 2009
Maps and graphics by Dianne Deudney

Editors
Lee Graham
Amber Tokeley

Consultant Editors
Dr Stephen Clarke, Royal New Zealand, Returned and Services' Association
Gary Oakley, Curator, Australian War Memorial
Olly Owen (completing doctoral studies at Oxford University)
Marika Sherwood, Senior Researcher, Institute of Commonwealth Studies
Captain Timothy C. Winegard, PhD (Oxford University)
Educational Advisor
Bea Lawes
  Haberdashers' Aske's Hatcham College

Design
Dianne Deudney

Cover Image of Luke Billings (age 18) wearing a RWAFF uniform
photography by Erick Myers.
Back cover photograph of Usain Bolt by Get Publishing and
  LCpl Ziaur Rahman, Westminster Dragoons Squadron,
  wearing a Burma Rifles Uniform photography by Emanuela Franchini.

All rights reserved. No reproduction, copy or transmission of this publication
may be made without written permission. No paragraph of this publication
may be reproduced, copied or transmitted save with written permission or in
accordance with the provisions of the Copyright, Design and Patents Act 1988,
or under the terms of any licence permitting limited copying issued by the
Copyright Licensing Agency, 90 Tottenham Court Road, London W1T 4LP.

The moral right of Erica Myers-Davis to be identified as copyright holder of
this work has been asserted by her in accordance with the Copyright, Design
and Patents Act 1988.

ISBN 978-0-9563919-0-2

This book is printed on paper suitable for recycling and made from fully
  managed and sustained forest sources.

A CIP catalogue record for this book is available from the British Library

Printed and bound in Great Britain by
The Colourhouse
  Arklow Road Trading Estate
  Arklow Road
  London SE14 6EB

CONTENTS

INTRODUCTION
Preface 4
Foreword 5
How to use this book 6
The British Empire and Commonwealth 8
World War II timeline 10
The Armed Forces during World War II 12

SECTION ONE
Australasia

UNIT 1: Australia 14
People Profiles
  Captain Reginald Saunders MBE 18
  Flight Sergeant Leonard Waters 20
  The Lovett Family 22
  Lance Corporal Kathleen Walker 24

UNIT 2: New Zealand 26
People Profiles
  Captain Nancy Wake AC, GM 32
  2nd Lieutenant Ngarimu VC 34
  Captain Keiha 35

UNIT 3: Pacific Islands 36
People Profiles
  Corporal Sefanaia Sukanaivalu VC 38
  Sir Jacob Charles Vouza GM, OBE 39

SECTION TWO
India and the Far East

UNIT 1: India 40
People Profiles
  Jemander Nand Singh VC, MVC 46
  Squadron Leader Majumdar DFC 48
  Asst Section Officer Khan GC 50

UNIT 2: Ceylon 52

UNIT 3: Malaya and British Singapore 53

UNIT 4: Burma 54
  Major Neville Hogan MBE 56

SECTION THREE
Africa

UNIT 1: Union of South Africa 60
People Profiles
  Lance Corporal Job Maseko MM 64
  Lance Corporal Lucas Majozi DCM 66

UNIT 2: British Southern Africa 68

UNIT 3: West Africa 72
People Profiles
  Major Seth Kwabla Anthony MSG, MBE 76
  Flying Officer John Henry Smythe OBE 78

UNIT 4:
East Africa 80

SECTION FOUR
West Indies

West Indies 84
People Profiles
  Flight Lieutenant Dudley Thompson 95
  Flight Lieutenant Cy Grant 96
  Squadron Leader Philip Louis Ulric Cross 98

SECTION FIVE
Canada

Canada
People Profiles 100
  Brigadier Oliver M Martin 106
  Flying Officer Gerry Bell 107
  Sergeant Tommy Prince 108

SECTION SIX
Activities

Activities 110
Index 118
Acknowledgements 119
Photography Credits 120
Puzzle solutions 120

PREFACE

ERICA MYERS-DAVIS
Author

I wrote this book to show the magnificent contribution made by those from the Commonwealth/British Empire in WWII, particularly as those of us from ethnic backgrounds are often portrayed in the annals of history as merely underdogs or oppressed.

My family is from Jamaica, I was born and raised in England and spent a third of my life in Australia, so I am a true citizen of the Commonwealth!

When I was a child, sadly, I was sometimes told 'to go back to where I came from' by ignorant people who had no knowledge of their history. But, alas, I had no knowledge of my heritage or history either. I didn't know that the West Indies had played a role in helping Great Britain remain British rather than fall to the dictators. Unfortunately the only history of the West Indies I learnt at school was about the Transatlantic Slave trade. Whilst that is part of our history, it was not balanced with stories of bravery, loyalty and courage which inspire rather than depress a child's mind and thinking.

This is a very special and unique book that you hold in your hands. Inside you will find people, events and activities that will inspire and encourage you, regardless of your heritage or background. No matter how large or small their contribution to the war effort, they did make a difference. What is even more astonishing is that despite the prejudice they sometimes experienced, they still chose to fight for Mother England. It has been a privilege and a pleasure to research the countless stories from around the world. Much information was sourced via the internet, libraries and museums, as well as through talking to veterans and veteran associations.

Finally, this book was inspired by and written for the Royal Commonwealth Ex-Services League, who will receive a royalty from book sales. The League, is a charity which provides financial assistance and support to veterans and their families from all parts of the Commonwealth who fought for the British Crown.

I hope this book will motivate you to do further research and ask questions of your elders and above all remember if you think you have no future, it's because you haven't understood your past.

Enjoy,

FOREWORD

HRH PRINCE HENRY OF WALES
Lieutenant, The Blues and Royals of the Household Cavalry Regiment

'Under One Flag' is an extremely important book, as it highlights the vital part indigenous and ethnic peoples of the Commonwealth played in securing victory in the Second World War.

The stories told in Under One Flag' are rarely heard, but they should be. The immense courage and selfless dedication of indigenous and ethnic peoples of what was then the British Empire deserve to be celebrated by us today. Those described in this book were ordinary people, but they rose to the challenges of extraordinary times so that we might live in peace and freedom.

Every year, The Royal Commonwealth Ex-Services League helps thousands of Commonwealth veterans and widows across the globe. The League's activities recognise the debt of gratitude we owe to these people and their matchless devotion to liberty.

I hope that everyone – whatever background you may have or ethnicity you may be – reading this book comes to share the same sense of pride that I feel, as a soldier and as someone who enjoys the freedoms that our predecessors fought for.

LANCE CORPORAL JOHNSON BEHARRY VC
Princess of Wales's Royal Regiment

Whilst I am very proud to be the first living recipient of the Victoria Cross since 1966, like everyone else profiled in this excellent book, Under One Flag, I was just doing my job.

Under One Flag shows the spirit and loyalty of indigenous and ethnic people of the Commonwealth who helped Great Britain win World War II. It charts the story of the Commonwealth contribution by highlighting individuals from across the globe. Not all of them are well-known or famous and I am delighted that they have been included.

I think this is one of the most important books on World War II for the classroom as it shows what an amazing contribution that people of colour have made. It also shows that frontline soldiers, of whatever colour, are accepted unreservedly by those with whom they serve. False values do not flourish amongst those fortunate enough to have experienced the close bond that servicemen and women of the British Armed Forces rely on every day.

I hope you enjoy this fascinating book as much as I did.

Standard Operating Procedures
How to use this book:

SECTIONS
The book is divided into five territories:

- Australasia
- India and Far East
- Africa
- West Indies
- Canada

You can easily find the section you want by looking for its colour on the right-hand side of the book when it is closed.

Each section features:
- The history and culture of the territory
- profiles of special military units or forces unique to that territory
- people profiles
- projects

Highlights unusual and interesting information

FACT FILE
The fact file gives important information which you can see at a glance

LANGUAGE
Some of the documents used in this book have been reproduced in their original form, keeping words and phrases in use at the time they were written.

Some of the words may refer to:
- ethnic or indigenous people
- countries or territories which were part of the British Empire
- military terms

which are no longer used today. Some words may be considered offensive in modern times.

They have been kept in the book in order to give a true picture of life and to highlight opinions held by some people at that time.

PEOPLE PROFILE
This gives detailed personal information about individual people.
D.O.B Date of birth
P.O.B Place of birth
D.O.D Date of death
Years of service in the Armed Forces
Rank The highest rank a person attained
Unit The group or unit the person belonged to
Engaagements Battles where they served
Awards Honours and awards they received
Other work Work they carried out in civilian life

TRIBUTES AND AWARDS
These boxes highlight tributes and awards

OPPOSING VIEWS AND QUOTES
These boxes highlight a point of view that differs or is a criticism.

MORSE CODE
Sending secret messages using codes or ciphers was (and still is) a vital part of wartime communication. At 160 years old, Morse Code is the oldest electronic encoding system in the world. A secret message in Morse Code for you to decode has been written at the bottom of each left-hand page throughout this book. The code can be found at the back of the book on page116.

MAPS

Maps at the begining of each section show important geographical features. There is also a large map in the introduction which shows all the countries in the British Empire at the time of the War.

NOTE: THE MAPS HAVE BEEN SIMPLIFIED AND ARE NOT TO SCALE

ICONS
These symbols identify activities or items of interest. Activities can be found on the Project cards in each section and also in the Activities section at the back of the book.

Debate or discuss
Research and explore the given topic

Re-enactment
Write a script or create and perform a piece of drama or dance

Investigate and report
Write a report a letter, or other document

Design, compose or construct
a piece of art or craft, a piece of creative writing or make something practical

Prisoners of war (POWs)
This symbol indicates that the serviceman or woman was imprisoned during the War.

Projects: For your eyes only

COVER STORY. These are fun activities you can do at school or at home, by yourself or in groups.

Introduction **7**

History of the British

FACT FILE

Dominion
Self-governing country

Colony
Country governed by Great Britain

Protectorate
Country which governs itself but is protected during war by a stronger country

Mandates
Countries given to Great Britain after World War I from the German and Ottoman Empires

Great Britain consists of only England, Scotland and Wales

UK is the United Kingdom of Great Britain and Northern Ireland

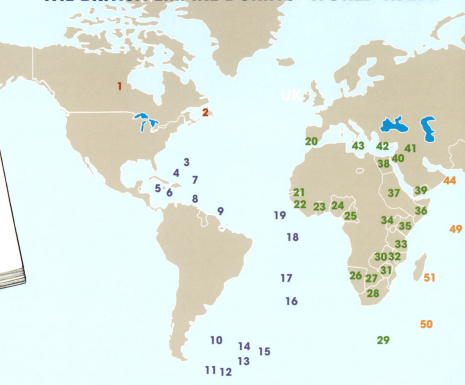

THE BRITISH EMPIRE DURING WORLD WAR II

The British Empire was made up of dominions, colonies, protectorates, mandates, and other territories ruled or administered by the United Kingdom. These originated from overseas colonies and trading posts established in the late 16th and early 17th centuries.

At its height, it was the largest empire in history and, for over 100 years, was the foremost global power. By 1922, the British Empire had a population of approximately 458 million people, one-quarter of the world's population, and covered more than 13,000,000 square miles (33,670,000 km²): about a quarter of the world's total land area. As a result, Great Britain's political, linguistic and cultural legacy is extensive.

It was often said that **"the sun never sets on the British Empire"** because its reach was so broad that there was always daylight in at least one of its numerous territories.

The economic and industrial growth of other countries such as Germany and the United States, along with the impact of World Wars I and II, placed enormous financial and political strain on Great Britain and its Empire. After World War II many of its colonies also saw a rise in the number of its citizens who wanted to break away from British rule. Indigenous people abd settlers actively sought decolonisation. During the latter half of the 20th century, most of the territories of the Empire became independent, ending with the return of Hong Kong to China in 1997. Many countries who gained their independence are now part of the Commonwealth. However there are still 14 territories that remain under British sovereignty today. These are now known as British Overseas Territories.

Commonwealth of Nations

The Commonwealth of Nations is also known as the Commonwealth or the British Commonwealth. Unlike the European Union, the Commonwealth is not a political union but a voluntary association of 53 independent

Empire and Commonwealth

Index

Canada:
1. Canada
2. Newfoundland

West Indies and South Atlantic:
3. Bermuda
4. Bahamas
5. British Honduras
6. Jamaica
7. West Indies
8. Trinidad
9. British Guiana
10. Falkland Islands
11. South Shetlands
12. Graham Land
13. South Orkneys
14. South Georgia
15. Sandwich Islands
16. Gough Island
17. Tristan da Cunha
18. St Helena
19. Ascension Island

Africa and the Mediterranean
20. Gibraltar
21. Gambia
22. Sierra Leone
23. Gold Coast
24. Nigeria
25. Cameroon
26. South West Africa
27. Bechuanaland
28. Union of South Africa
29. Prince Edward Island
30. Northern Rhodesia
31. Southern Rhodesia
32. Nyasaland
33. Kenya
34. Uganda
35. Tanganyika
36. British Somaliland
37. Anglo Egyptian Sudan
38. Egypt
39. Aden
40. Transjordan
41. Iraq
42. Cyprus
43. Malta

India, Indian Ocean and Far East
44. Socotra
45. India
46. Celon
47. Chagos
48. Diego Garcia
49. Seychelles
50. Crozet Island
51. Mauritius
52. Burma
53. Malaya
54. Singapore
55. Borneo
56. Hong Kong
57. Kaiser Wilhelm's Island
58. Wei Hei Wei
59. Papua
60. Naura
61. Gilbert islands
62. Ellice Islands
63. Fiji

Australasia
64. Australia
65. New Zealand

member states. The British monarch is the Head of the Commonwealth. This is a ceremonial position, which means that he or she takes an advisory role and acts as the chief representative at special occasions. Day-to-day activities are undertaken by an administrative unit called the Commonwealth Secretariat. All states are regarded as equal in status and work together towards common values and goals such as:

- democracy
- human rights
- good governance
- the rule of law
- individual liberty
- free trade
- world peace

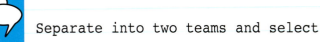

Project: For your eyes only

```
Separate into two teams and select
a British Empire country.
Team 1 will represent the British Government.
Team 2 will represent the indigenous
         population/Administration.
Team 1 Create an argument in favour of keeping the
         colony under British control.
Team 2 Create an argument in favour of independence
         from Great Britain.
```

Introduction 9

World War II timeline

Seven British Empire military personnel in uniform marching under the Union Jack.
From left to right there is a West African soldier in a slouch hat; a British soldier in a pith helmet; an Indian soldier wearing a turban; a Canadian airman in blue uniform; a New Zealand soldier in a 'lemon squeezer' slouch hat; an Australian soldier in a slouch hat; and a sailor of the Royal Navy in a dark blue naval uniform.

IWM/PST3158

World War II was the most devastating event in human history. More than 100 million people fought and in excess of 70 million people (mainly civilians) were killed.

The War had a global impact on economies, industries, scientific advances and political beliefs. Importantly, it positively impacted on the status and role of women and ethnic minorities who had previously experienced prejudice by the white, male, ruling classes. For example, many women were able to do jobs that had previously been performed by men, while some ethnic minorities who enlisted in the armed forces experienced equality for the first time.

FACT FILE
The two opposing military alliances of the War are called the Allies and the Axis.

Allies
British Empire
United States of America
Union of Soviet Socialist Republics

Axis
Germany
Italy
Japan

1936

7 March
Germany occupies Rhineland

9 May
Italy annexes (takes over) Abyssinia

17 July
Spanish Civil War commences

25 November
Japan and Germany sign Anti-comintern pact

1937

28 May
Neville Chamberlain becomes British Prime Minister

1938

11 March
Anschluss – Germany annexes Austria

9 November
Kristallnacht – Night of Broken Glass: Jews and their property are targeted and attacked in Germany

1939

31 March
France and Great Britain guarantee to protect Poland's territorial borders

1 April
End of Spanish Civil War

26 April
Compulsory conscription introduced in Great Britain

22 May
Italy and Germany sign the 'Pact of Steel'

1 September
Germany invades Poland

3 September
France and Great Britain declare war on Germany

27 September
Fall of Warsaw

4 November
US Congress passes Neutrality Act

10

1940

9 April
Germany invades Denmark and Norway

10 May
Germany invades the Netherlands, Belgium and France

Winston Churchill becomes British Prime Minister

26 May – 4 June
British retreat from Dunkirk

28 May
Surrender of Belgian Army

10 June
Italy declares war on France and Great Britain

14 June
Germans enter Paris

22 June
France signs an armistice with Germany

21 June
Italy attacks France

24 June
France signs an armistice with Italy

28 June
Great Britain recognises de Gaulle as head of the 'Free French'

10 July
Start of the Battle of Britain

4 August
Italian troops invade British Somaliland

12 September
Italian invasion of Egypt

28 October
Italy attacks Greece

27 September
Germany, Japan and Italy sign the Tripartite Pact

1941

19 January
Britain launches an offensive in East Africa

24 April
Beginning of British evacuation of Greece

7 December
Japanese attack Pearl Harbor

8 December
USA and Great Britain declare war on Japan

11 December
Italy and Germany declare war on USA

1942

15 February
Japanese capture Singapore

19 February
Japanese air raid on Port Darwin, Australia

21 June
Rommel captures Tobruk

1 July
Beginning of the First Battle of El Alamein

9 August
Start of a 'civil disobedience' campaign against British rule in India

24 October
Beginning of the Second Battle of El Alamein

8 November
Allied troops land in Africa

2 February
Germans surrender at Stalingrad

1943

13 February
First Chindit operation in Burma

3 May
Allies capture Tunis

13 May
Surrender of Axis forces in North Africa

25 July
Mussolini is overthrown and arrested. A new government is formed under Marshal Badoglio

13 October
Italy declares war on Germany

1944

15 February
Beginning of Japanese offensive on the border between India and Burma

6 June
D-Day, Allied landings in Normandy

25 August
Germans surrender in Paris

1945

28 April
Mussolini is shot by members of the Resistance

30 April
Hitler commits suicide with wife Eva Braun in his bunker

3 May
British capture Rangoon

4-5 May
German forces surrender in the Netherlands, northern Germany, Denmark and Norway

7 May
Jodl signs unconditional German surrender at Reims

8 May
V-E Day (Victory in Europe)

6 August
US drops first atomic bomb on Hiroshima, Japan

9 August
US drops second atomic bomb on Nagasaki, Japan

14 August
Emperor Hirohito announces unconditional surrender of Imperial Japanese forces

14-15 August
V-J Day (Victory over Japan)

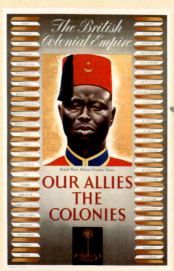

IWM/PST8262

A British poster paying tribute to the support from the colonies, featuring a head and shoulder portrait of a member of the RWAFF (see page 74) in uniform and below is the RWAFF's regimental badge. A list of all Great Britain's colonies runs down the left and right of the poster.

Introduction **11**

The Armed Forces during World

Uniforms and equipment
Two Chindit soliders (see page 44) Burma Rifles Scout (left) Royal West African Frontier F

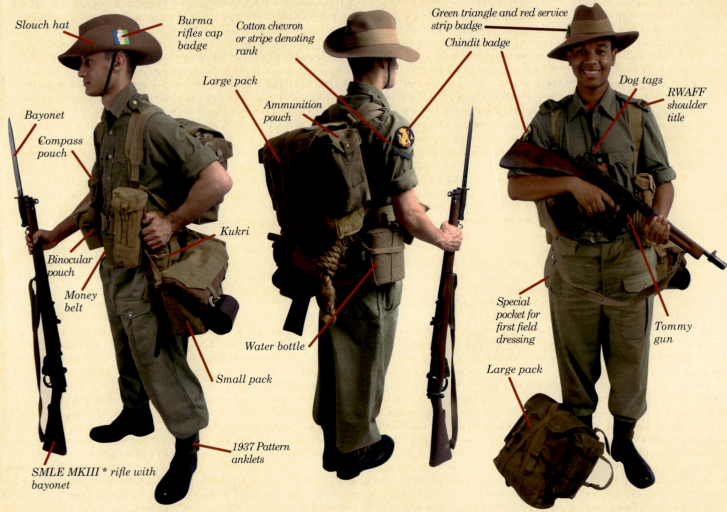

Here are two examples of Commonwealth soldiers' uniforms and equipment. On the left is a Burma Rifles scout and on the right is a Royal West African soldier Both the Burma Rifles and the RWAFF served as part of a special unit called the Chindits (see page 44) in Burma. The soldiers carried between 55lb and 70lb of kit and marched between 20 to 80 miles a day. Their shirts were made from a cotton fabric called Airtex which allowed sweat to be absorbed, keeping the body cool. Their Indian Jungle Green Battledress trousers were made from a heavy duty cotton called Drill.

Weapons

Lee-Enfield rifle, the SMLE Mk III* and could fire a .303 calibre round. EM

Sten MkII submachine gun
Fired a 9mm Parabellum round at 500rpm. The gun was very cheap to produce but was disliked because of its ability to fire if dropped (when cocked). However it became used throughout the world during WWII. MOT

The Thompson submachine gun was an American submachine gun, invented by John T Thompson in 1919 and was also known informally as the 'Tommy Gun'. In the Far East, British Empire and Commonwealth forces initially used Tommy guns extensively in jungle patrols and ambushes, where it was prized for its firepower. However its hefty weight of over 10lb (4.5kg) and difficulties in supply eventually led to its replacement by other submachine guns such as the Sten gun. EM

War I

- Slouch hat
- Indian 'Dah' machete aka parang
- Crossover webbing
- Leather sleeve for parang
- Entrenching tool
- Bayonet
- Toggle and rope
- Small pack
- Tin mug
- Black leather boots

EM

During WWII identity discs, also known as dog tags, contained a soldier's name, number and religion. The disc shown right belonged to an officer S R Tierney, OFFR 222129 CE
EM

The Kukri, or Gurkha knife, could be used to clear a path through the jungle as well as to attack enemies. The smaller knives pictured are used for sharpening the Kukri and skinning animals. When not in use they are placed inside a small sheath behind the main scabbard. EM

THE GALLANTRY GALLERY

The Victoria Cross (VC) and George Cross (GC) are the two highest military decorations awarded for valour and great bravery. They may be awarded to a person of any rank in any service or to civilians under military command.

Victoria Cross
Awarded for most conspicuous bravery or act of valour or self-sacrifice, or for extreme devotion to duty in the presence of an enemy.

Description
Bronze Cross Pattée with Crown and Lion superimposed and the motto 'For Valour'
Postnominals: VC

George Cross
Awarded for acts of conspicuous gallantry performed by men or women when not in the face of the enemy.

Description
Plain silver cross with circular medallion in the centre depicting the effigy of St. George and the Dragon, surrounded by the words 'For Gallantry'.
Postnominals: GC

Typical Army Structure in WWII

Below is the basic structure of the British Army during WWII; most Commonwealth armies followed this structure.

	Organisations	Consisting of	Commanded by
FORMATIONS	Army	2 or more corps	General
	Corps	2 or more divisions	Lieutenant General
	Division	3 brigades	Major General
	Brigade	3 battalions	Brigadier (General)
UNITS	Battalion	4 companies	Lieutenant Colonel
	Company	3 platoons	Captain or Major
	Platoon	3 sections	Lieutenant
	Section		Corporal/Sergeant

RANKS
The most senior rank is at the top, with the most junior rank at the bottom.

Commissioned officers

NAVY	ARMY	AIRFORCE
Admiral of the Fleet	Field Marshal	Marshal of the Air Force
Admiral	General	Air Chief Marshal
Vice-Admiral	Lieutenant General	Air Marshal
Rear-Admiral	Major General	Air Vice Marshal
Commodore	Brigadier	Air Commodore
Captain	Colonel	Group Captain
Commander	Lieutenant Colonel	Wing Commander
Lieutenant-Commander	Major	Squadron Leader
Lieutenant	Captain	Flight Lieutenant
Sub-Lieutenant	Lieutenant	Flight Officer
Commissioned Warrant Officer	Second Lieutenant	Pilot Officer

Non-commissioned ranks (NCO)

SEAMAN	SOLDIERS	AIRMEN
Warrant Officer	Regimental Sergeant Major	Warrant Officer Class 1
	Company Sergeant Major	Warrant Officer Class 2
Chief Petty Officer	Staff/Colour Sergeant	Flight Sergeant
Petty Officer	Sergeant	Sergeant
Leading Rate	Corporal	Corporal
Able Seaman	Lance Corporal	Leading Aircraftsman
Ordinary Seaman	Private	Aircraftman

Introduction 13

SECTION 1 AUSTRALASIA
Unit 1: Australia

Australia is an island continent. The country of Australia is therefore also the continent of Australia.

In this unit we are going to explore the indigenous people who served as ANZACs (see factfile right).

The ANZACs played a key role in both World War I and World War II. Between 1939 and 1945 nearly one million service personnel fought in defence of Great Britain. They left their homelands to fight in Europe, Asia and North Africa. Back home the Australian 'Diggers' also had to defend their country against invasion by the Japanese.

In 1770 the British took possession of Australia. The indigenous people, also known as Aboriginals and Torres Strait Islanders, had their land and rights removed. Aboriginals typically lived a 'hunter-gatherer' lifestyle. Many tribes moved around from place to place, with all living off the land. The 18th century Britons who took over this land viewed this lifestyle as primitive.

Aboriginals also had a radically different concept of ownership: they believed that they were caretakers of the land, rather owners. They believed that the plants, animals and people belonged to the land, unlike the British who believed that the land and everything in it belonged to those who claimed it first.

By 1788, the British had become established in Australia, and 40,000 years of traditional life for the Aboriginal peoples changed for ever. In the fight for land, thousands of indigenous people were killed, forcibly removed from their land, disenfranchised and forced to live in squalor.

Two Aboriginals demonstrate to an Australian soldier the art of spear throwing in Darwin c. 1942
AWM012851

Melville Islanders enlisted in the Royal Australian Navy for special duties such as locating stranded airmen and Japanese mines (see next page, Special Units.) AWM062344

Australia became a penal colony, meaning that the British transported their criminals and convicts to jails which they had built. Once these convicts had gained their freedom they were given more rights than the indigenous inhabitants of the country. Various settlements were established around the continent which, between 1855 and 1890, became six self-governing colonies while remaining part of the British Empire. In 1901 the federation of the colonies was achieved and the Commonwealth of Australia was born as a Dominion of the British Empire. Constitutional links between Australia and Britain formally ended in 1931 although Australia did not adopt the Statute of Westminster until 1942 which granted legal and political independence to Commonwealth countries.

On 3rd September 1939 Australia's Prime Minister Robert Menzies formally announced Australia's involvement in the war.

Unfortunately it is difficult to know exactly how many people of Aboriginal descent were ANZACs as records from the time do not list ethnicity. During the War Aboriginals lived on missions, very much like the reservations for indigenous people in North America. They were not allowed to leave these missions without permission from the local police chief. Some ran away from these missions crossing state borders and changing their names in the process. All who enlisted did so voluntarily. At this time the Australian Census failed to include Aboriginals in their records. In fact indigenous people were legally excluded from it, until the 1967 Referendum.

Researchers from the Australian War Memorial estimate that around 3,000 indigenous people volunteered during World War II to serve in uniform as part of the Defence Force proper, though the true number will never be known. While this may seem a small figure, the indigenous population at the time may have accounted for just 70 000 people or 1% of the total population of Australia.

FACT FILE
1939 Australian Population — 6,998,000
Military deaths — 40,500
Civilian deaths due to war — 700
ANZAC — Australian New Zealand Army Corp
Call sign — The Diggers
ANZAC Day — 25 April
Victoria Cross medals — 20
Engagements
Germany
Italy
The Mediterranean
North Africa
South East Asia and other parts of the Pacific
North West Australian mainland
Midget Submarines in Sydney Harbour

Victoria Cross

THE ABORIGINAL FLAG

This was designed by Harold Thomas in 1971, an Aboriginal artist from Central Australia. There are many explanations for the use of the colours, but the commonest is that red represents the earth and the blood spilt, black represents the night sky and the skin of the people, and the gold disc is the sun -- giver of all life.

Australia 15

Group portrait of the ship's company of the stores carrier HMAS Matafele, a British ship which was later commissioned by the Royal Australian Navy. She was lost with all hands between Townsville and Milne Bay on 18 June 1944. AWM/305321

At an undisclosed operational base in Darwin, indigenous service personnel use a camel team to transport supplies to an allied outpost. AWM/013025

Despite being treated as second-class citizens, many Aboriginals volunteered to defend their country on behalf of the war effort, both at home and abroad.

The Australian Army, Royal Australian Air Force and the Royal Australian Navy had rules stating that anyone who did not have a European background could not enlist with them prior to the start of World War II.

==Many Aboriginal soldiers got round this by saying that they had Maori or Indian heritage.==

However, the threat of Japanese invasion forced the military to allow the enlistment of Aboriginal and Torres indigenous people and other Islanders in 1941. There were some special units made up of indigenous personnel who stayed to defend the home front, whilst many others were sent overseas to fight alongside their white colleagues.

SPECIAL UNITS

Northern Territory Special Reconnaissance Unit

These soldiers used their traditional bushcraft and fighting skills to patrol the coastal areas and established coastwaters, and to fight a guerrilla war against any Japanese who landed.

Members lived off the land, used traditional weapons, were mobile and had no supply line to protect. This unit received no monetary pay until back pay and medals were finally awarded in 1992. Fifty tribal Yolngu men from Eastern Arnhem Land were trained to defend the northern coastline of Australia from Japanese attack using traditional weapons.

Their role was to provide the city of Darwin with an early warning of a Japanese attack. They were paid three sticks of tobacco per week. Prior to the war, some of these men had been jailed for killing Japanese pearlers.

Torres Strait Island Light Infantry Battalion

Around 750 Torres Strait Islanders and 60 mainland Murri people defended the Torres Strait, a vital shipping route connecting Darwin with Australia's east coast. Islanders in the Battalion were paid one-third of the rate of their non-indigenous colleagues. This was finally rectified in 1983. **In proportion to population, no community in Australia contributed more to the war effort than the Torres Strait Islanders.**

Defence of Bathurst and Melville Islands

Wearing navy uniforms and armed and equipped by the Royal Australian Navy, 35 Tiwi people from Melville Islands patrolled Melville and Bathurst Islands. They served from 1942 to 1945 but were never formally enlisted or paid a wage.

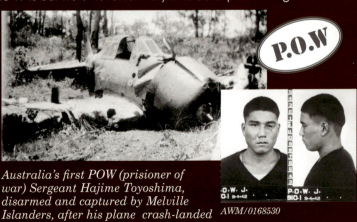

Australia's first POW (prisoner of war) Sergeant Hajime Toyoshima, disarmed and captured by Melville Islanders, after his plane crash-landed during Japan's first attack on Darwin. AWM/013025

AWM/0168530

16

P.O.W

Informal portrait of two Aboriginal servicemen Private (Pte.) Frederick Beale (left) and his brother Pte. George Beale (right) with Pte. Michael (Joe) Lynch, all of the 2/20th Battalion.
All three were captured, and became POWs in Singapore after its fall on 15 February 1942. Both Pte. Beales spent time in Changi before being forced to work as steel mill labourers in Japan. Pte. Lynch was transported to Thailand and worked on the Burma-Thai Railway (see page 55).
Pte. George Beale died on the operating table from injuries sustained in an accident after working a 24 hour shift in May 1943. His brother was released just four months later. AWM/PO/649.002

Indigenous Australians have fought for Australia and the British Crown since the Boer War in 1902.

While serving in the armed forces, most experienced equality for the first time in their lives. However, in civilian life, they were still often subjected to discrimination and prejudice.

During WWII indigenous Australians
- could not vote
- were not counted on the census
- could not own land they had traditionally inhabited
- were not full citizens of Australia
- adults could not drink in local pubs with their white compatriots

WHY DID THEY FIGHT?
- **Loyalty**
- **Patriotism** For 'my country'
- **Bravery** To prove that they were still warriors
- **Opportunity** For some it was simply a chance to receive good, regular pay and a trip overseas
- **A belief** that they would gain their civil liberties
- **A sense of pride**

William Cooper, Secretary of the Australian Aborigines' League, once said:

"Aborigines should not fight for White Australia."

He argued that the whites' treatment of Aboriginals was the same as Hitler's treatment of the Jews. Cooper demanded improvements at home for his people, before they sacrificed themselves to defend the land which was forcibly taken from them by the whites.

THE TORRES STRAIT FLAG

The Torres Strait Islander flag was designed in 1992 by Bernard Namok. The green stripes at the top and bottom of the flag symbolise the land and the blue stripe in the centre repesents the waters of the Torres Strait. The thin, black stripes and the white headdress represent the Islanders. The white, five-pointed star represents the five major island groups.

Project: For your eyes only

COVER STORY.
Operation Join Now
You are a recruiting officer for the Australian Armed Forces. Design an advertising campaign to recruit Aboriginals into the Army, Navy or Air Force. What would be the best way to reach them? Would you use newspapers, radio, cinema, posters or other media? Design posters, radio and cinema ads, write a newspaper article. How else could you reach them?

Australia

PEOPLE PROFILES Captain Reginald Walter Saunders MBE

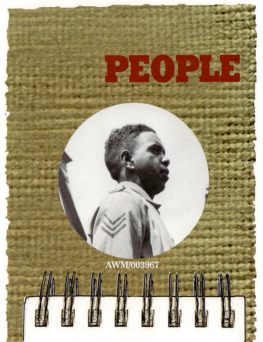
AWM/003967

FACT FILE
First Aboriginal commissioned officer in the Australian Army.
D.O.B 7 August 1920
Framlingham, Victoria
D.O.D 2 March 1990
Sydney, New South Wales
Years of service
1940—1954
Rank Captain
Unit 2/7th Battalion
3rd Battalion
Engagements
World War II
North African Campaign
Battle of Greece
Battle of Crete
New Guinea Campaign
Salamaua-Lae Campaign
Korean War
Battle of Kapyong
Awards
Member of the Order of the British Empire (MBE)
Other work
Office of Aboriginal Affairs as a liaison and public relations officer

Captain Saunders, a member of the Aboriginal Gunditjmara tribe, followed in the footsteps of his father and uncle who had both fought in France in World War I.

Saunders enlisted on 24 April 1940 and, after his initial training, proved to be a natural soldier. He also found less discrimination in the Australian Army than in the wider community.

He was a popular member of the 2/7th Battalion. His unit saw action in North Africa before joining the ill-fated Greek campaign. After Greece, his unit fought on Crete, and when the Allies evacuated in May 1941, Saunders was one of many men left behind. He was forced to remain hidden on the island for a year, helped by locals, before being rescued by the British Navy.

Saunders returned to Australia before rejoining his battalion in New Guinea as a sergeant. In mid-1944 his commanding officer nominated him for officer training. He was commissioned in November 1944 and returned to New Guinea. For the remainder

Souvenir Pennant of the 2/7th Battalion that belonged to Reg Saunders; it bears badges collected during his service in World War II and Korea.
It also includes recognition from the USA in the form of the 'US Presidential Unit Citation.'
AWM/RELAWM320920

Saunders and 'Diver' Derrick graduated from an Officer Cadet Training Unit in November 1944. AWM/083166

of the War he was a platoon commander in New Guinea.

After the war he returned to Australia and worked as a shipping clerk and builder's labourer.

Saunders returned to the Army at the outbreak of the Korean War, where he served as a Captain of the 3rd Battalion, Royal Australian Regiment and fought at Kapyong. This battalion won a United States Presidential Citation for the Battle of Kapyong.

On leaving the army he had difficulty settling into

Sgt. Saunders on leave from New Guinea. "He was accepted unreservedly by the men who served with him. He was respected and popular among his men. not flourish among front-line soldiers," said Harry Gordon, biographer and journalist
AWM/057894

civilian life, particularly as an indigenous man living among white people. He worked through these difficulties by becoming a spokesperson for indigenous Australians. In 1969 Saunders joined the Office of Aboriginal Affairs as a liaison and public relations officer in an effort to make life better for his people.

He travelled all over the country meeting indigenous people from all walks of life. He died in Sydney in 1990, leaving behind eight children.

Saunders' uncle William Reginald Rawlings, received the Military Medal for his service with the First Australian Imperial Force. His brother Harry also enlisted for service in World War II. He was later killed in New Guinea.

In 1971 Captain Saunders was made a Member of the Order of the British Empire.

Project: For your eyes only

"He was accepted unreservedly by the men who served with him because false values do not flourish among front-line soldiers." What does this quote mean? What does it tell you about Saunders' character?

Design and make a souvenir pennant for Captain Saunders or another person profiled in this book.

THE GUNDITJMARA

In the early days when the British first arrived in Australia the Gunditjmara fought many battles with the white settlers in an attempt to keep their land.

Unit 1 Australia 19

PEOPLE PROFILES Flight Sergeant Leonard V Waters

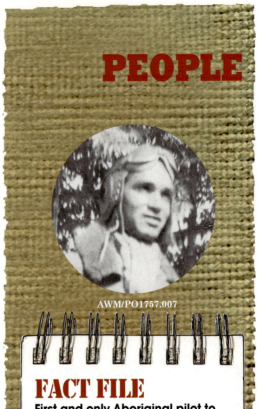

AWM/PO1757.007

FACT FILE

First and only Aboriginal pilot to serve in the Royal Australian Air Force (RAAF) during World War II

D.O.B 29 June 1924 Boomi
P.O.B New South Wales
D.O.D 24 August 1993 Cunnamulla, Queensland

Years of Service
1942—1946
Rank Warrant officer
Unit No. 78 Squadron RAAF
Engagements
World War II
Awards
Dutch War Commemorative Cross 1940-1945
Other work
Sheep shearer

Flight Sergeant Waters grew up admiring pioneering aviators Charles Kingsford-Smith and Amy Johnson.

At the age of 13, Waters had to leave school to work with his father as a ringbarker in the forests to support his family of 11 children. He was paid less than one-sixth of the average wage at the time. Three years later, in 1939, he became a sheep shearer.

Officially, those of Aboriginal descent could not enlist in the military. But once Japan entered the War and Australia became a target, these restrictions were lifted. The RAAF in particular was less restrictive as it required huge numbers of personnel.

Many Aboriginals and Islanders were employed for patrol duty and to rescue downed pilots in Northern Australia. This allowed Leonard Waters to volunteer for service in the RAAF in Brisbane on 24 August 1942.

Initially he started training as an aircraft mechanic but later volunteered for the aircrew service and was accepted. Waters began his training in 1943 and received his 'wings;' this means that he qualified as a pilot.

> "I was terribly keen to prove myself in the elite... [and] the flying part of the Air Force is the elite. I might add that there were 375 [students] on that course and 48 of us finished up as pilots..."
> Len Waters

Waters graduated in the top five of his class.

On 14 November 1944 he was posted to No. 78 Squadron, a fighter unit based on Noemfoor, an island off Dutch New Guinea (West Papua). Here he was allocated a P-40 Kittyhawk.

The previous pilot had nicknamed the plane 'Black Magic' and had painted the words on its nose. Waters chose to keep the name. No.78 Squadron's main role was ground attack, and Waters flew 95 sorties from Noemfoor and later from various airbases in Borneo.

On 1 January 1945 he was promoted to flight sergeant, and by the end of the war he was commanding operations.

During his time with the air force Waters held the RAAF middleweight boxing title. On 18 January 1946 he finally

20 — .... --- ..- ... .- -. -.. ...

In Morotai 1945, Flight Sergeant Waters relaxes in the squadron's tent lines with bottles of 'jungle juice' (home brewed alcohol), left over from his 21st birthday party the night before.
AWM/PO1757.005

left the RAAF with the rank of warrant officer. After the War he hoped to find a career in flying and even tried to establish an airline service in Queensland but the Australian government ignored his requests. He didn't fly a plane again and eventually returned to shearing. Sadly for him, civilian life did not allow him to use the valuable skills he had gained during the War.

Waters died, aged 69, in Cunnamulla and was buried in St. George Cemetery.

His brother, Donald Edward (Jim) Waters, served as an infantryman with the Australian Army.

AWARDS

- Waters was awarded the Dutch War Commemorative Cross 1940-1945
- There are two memorial parks dedicated to him in Inala, Queensland, and Boggabill, New South Wales.
- A street in Ngunnawal, Australian Capital Terrority, has been named Len Waters Street.
- In 1995, Waters' war service was commemorated with the issue of a postage stamp by Australia Post.

This material has been reproduced with permission of the Australian Postal Corporation. The original work is held in the National Philatelic Collection.

- More recently, in 2003, a monument was erected to his memory in St. George.

Project: For your eyes only

COVER STORY.
You are a pilot in No.78 Squadron, RAAF. You fly the Curtiss P-40 N-15 Kittyhawk. Your aircraft is nicknamed 'Black Magic'. Recent intelligence has revealed that the enemy, the Imperial Japanese Army Air Force, fly the Kawasaki Ki-61 Hien, codenamed 'Tony'. To better understand your enemy's possible tactics, you need to find out all you can about this aircraft and see how it compares to yours.

Describe the best and worst features of the two aircraft. It will be helpful to draw or get photos of each aircraft. Who are the designers? Where are the aircraft manufactured? How easy will it be to shoot and destroy 'Tony'? Which attack tactics will the enemy use against you? How can you protect your squadron?

Waters receives his 'wings' during his graduation ceremony
AWM/PO1757.004

Australia 21

PEOPLE PROFILES The Lovett Family

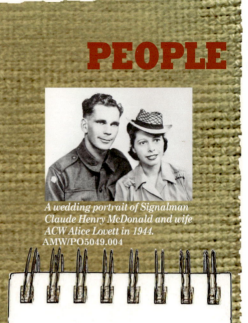

A wedding portrait of Signalman Claude Henry McDonald and wife ACW Alice Lovett in 1944.
AMW/PO5049.004

FACT FILE

The Lovett family belong to the Gunditjmara people in Victoria, Australia.

Hannah and James Lovett saw five of their twelve children serve overseas in World War I — Alfred, Leonard, Edward, Frederick and Herbert.

In World War II, Samuel, Edward, Frederick and Herbert fought abroad whilst Leonard, Alfred and another older brother served in garrisons and in the catering units in Australia. A nephew, Robert served in the Air Force.

Their grandchildren, Alice and Pearl, served in World War II, three others served in Korea and one grandson was with the British Commonwealth Occupation Force in post-war Japan. Alice's son, Mervyn McDonald, served in Vietnam. In 1999 Frederick's grandson, Ricky Morris, served with Peacekeeping Forces in East Timor.

No other family achieved so much in service to the Commonwealth.

Aircraftwoman (ACW) Alice Lovett, daughter of Private Leonard Lovett, served with the WAAAF. Before enlisting in 1941 she worked as a domestic servant and nanny. She excelled in her work and was offered a promotion to corporal in 1942. She turned it down as it meant she would have to move to Queensland, which was too far away from family and friends.

Shortly after, she resigned from the WAAAF and joined friends working at a local munitions factory in Maribyrnong. She married her husband Claude McDonald in 1944, who served with the 10th Australian Despatch Radar Section in New Guinea, Torakina and Bougainville from 1941 until the end of the War.

Years later their son Mervyn went to fight in Vietnam. Alice's father also served as a guard at a prisoner-of-war camp in Murchison. Private Lovett previously had a German singing teacher and could speak the language fluently. The POWs he guarded were young Germans captured from submarines.

Since World War II, other Lovett family members have served in Korea, Vietnam and more recently in East Timor.

Twenty members of the family have seen service across both World Wars, as well as in Japan, Korea, Vietnam and East Timor.

The Lake Condah Mission, the Gunditjmara's ancestral land where the Lovett brothers grew up, was carved into soldier-settlement blocks after World War II.

"But my father didn't receive any block— him or his brothers,"

Pte. Alfred Lovett of the 6th Reinforcements of the 26th Battalion with his wife, Sarah, and their two sons in 1915. AWM/PO165

Pte. Leonard Lovett (father of Alice), 39th Battalion in 1919.
AWM/PO1651

22

SPECIAL UNIT

according to Johnnie Lovett, Herbert's son. "When he'd finished his service for this country, he was given nothing."

The Women's Auxiliary Australian Air Force (WAAAF) was the first and largest of the World War II Australian women's services formed in February 1941. It led to the formation of other women's service organisations such as The Australian Women's Army Service (AWAS) and the Women's Royal Australian Naval Service (WRANS).
The key role of the WAAAF was to provide skilled and semi-skilled signals and maintenance workers for the Royal Australian Air Force so that the men could serve abroad.

Australian Rules football player Nathan Lovett-Murray is the great grandson of Frederick Lovett.

TRIBUTES

Nigel Steel, the chief historian at London's Imperial War Museum, told the Australian Broadcasting Corporation that he knew of no service record to match the Lovetts.'

On 31 May 2000 Canberra's tallest building was officially renamed Lovett Tower, in their honour.

Pte. Samuel Lovett of 6th Reinforcements, 2/5 Battalion with his niece, ACW Alice Lovett, who is wearing 1942 pattern WAAAF overalls.
AWM/PO1651.003

Pte. Samuel Lovett in Palestine 1941.
AWM/PO1651.002

Project: For your eyes only

COVER STORy.
You are a younger member of an indigenous family who was left behind when your cousins joined the war effort.

Make ANZAC Biscuits (see recipe in the Activities section) to send to your cousins on the front line.

Servicemen, probably from the 10th Australian Despatch Radar Section. Signalman Claude Henry McDonald, Alice Lovett's husband, is at the back, left.
AWM/PO5049.003

Australia **23**

PEOPLE PROFILES Lance Corporal Kathleen Mary Joan Walker

AWM/PO1688.001

FACT FILE

Communications worker with the Australian Women's Army Service (AWAS) and a political activist. Her later work helped to achieve full citizenship rights for indiginous people. She was the first Aboriginal Australian to publish a book of poetry.

D.O.B 3 November 1920
P.O.B Minjerribah (Stradbroke Island), Queensland
D.O.D 16 September 1993
Awards Member of the British Empire (MBE)
Other work
   Domestic servant
   Poet
   Author

Kathleen Walker was a member of the Noonuccal people and one of six children.

Walker left school at 13 at the height of the Depression and got work as a domestic servant. At 16 she was rejected for nurse's training because she was Aboriginal. Despite this she still volunteered for service in the AWAS (see right). She worked as a communications worker at Army HQ in Brisbane and reached the rank of Lance Corporal.

During her service in the AWAS, Walker noticed that for the first time in her life she ws treated the same as white people. She also learned a lot from meeting and working with African American soldiers.

After the War she worked again as a domestic servant and also joined the Communist Party of Australia, which was the only political party opposed to treating Aboriginals as second-class citizens. She was a key figure in successfully lobbying the Government. She spoke to two Prime Ministers, Robert Menzies and his successor Harold Holt, who later decided to reform the Australian constitution to allow Aboriginal people full citizenship.

Walker wrote many books and won several awards for them (see right.) She was awarded an MBE in 1970.

In 1988 she reclaimed her traditional name, Oodgeroo Noonuccal (pronounced Ood-gerr-rooh Nooh-nuh-cal) and returned her MBE to protest at how the Aboriginals were treated during the year of Australia's bicenterary celebrations. Oodgeroo Noonuccal died in 1993, aged 73.

The Australian Women's Army Service or **AWAS** was a non-medical women's service formed in 1941 by Miss Sybil Howy Irving MBE, who was given the rank of lieutenant colonel. Prior to this commission, Lieutenant Colonel Irving had received an MBE for her work as secretary of the Girl Guide's Association in Victoria.

The AWAS was established so that women could take on certain jobs while men went out to fight. These included:

- clerks
- orderlies
- cooks
- drivers
- signallers
- communication workers
- anti-aircraft defence personnel

*An AWAS recruitment poster.
LHQ Lithographic Coy,
Australian Survey Corps;
McCowan, Ian; Unknown
A.W.A.S wants 100s of Australia's keenest
women urgently..., 1941-1945 (Date printed);
1941-1945 (Date published)
photolithograph 61.2 x 47.6 cm
Australian War Memorial (ARTV00335)*

! We need help, not exploitation,
We want freedom, not frustration;
Not control, but self-reliance,
Independence, not compliance.

(Aboriginal Charter of Rights)

WALKER'S AWARDS

- Mary Gilmore Medal
- Jessie Litchfield Award
- International Acting Award
- Fellowship of Australian Writers' Award
- Member British Empire
- Honorary Doctorate (Macquarie University)
- Doctorate (Griffith University)

Project: For your eyes only

COVER STORY. You are a poet and artist.

Write a poem describing life as an Aboriginal woman before, during and after the War. Illustrate it in Aboriginal patterns and colours, as shown here.

The Coloured Digger

*He came and joined the colours,
when the War God's anvil rang,*

*He took up modern weapons
to replace his boomerang,*

*He waited for no call-up,
he didn't need a push,*

*He came in from the stations,
and the townships of the bush.*

*He helped when help was wanting,
just because he wasn't deaf;*

*He is right amongst the columns
of the fighting A.I.F.*

*He is always there when wanted,
with his Owen gun or Bren,*

*He is in the forward area,
the place where men are men.*

*He proved he's still a warrior,
in action not afraid,*

*He faced the blasting red-hot fire
from mortar and grenade;*

*He didn't mind when food was low,
or we were getting thin,*

*He didn't growl or worry then
he'd cheer us with his grin.*

*He'd heard us talk democracy,
They preach it to his face,*

*Yet knows that in our Federal House
there's no one of his race.*

*He feels we push his kinsmen out,
here cities do not reach,*

*And Parliament has yet to hear
the Aborigine's maiden speech.*

*One day he'll leave the Army,
then join the League he shall,*

*And he hopes we'll give a better deal
to the Aboriginal.*

(This poem, by Sapper Bert Beros, a non-Aboriginal soldier in World War II was written about Private West—one of his Aboriginal comrades)

Australia **25**

SECTION 1 AUSTRALASIA
Unit 2: New Zealand

New Zealand is the youngest country on Earth, with the first settlers arriving from Polynesia some time in the 13th century. They brought with them a rich oral history, made tools, weapons and ornaments, hunted food and cultivated crops. They developed Maori culture which is focused on family, land and the connection between the two. Some areas of the islands were unsuitable for horticulture and some animals were hunted to extinction, which increased fighting between tribes.

The Dutch were the first Europeans to discover New Zealand in 1642 and the British mapped the islands in 1769-70. This marked the arrival of traders, sealers, whalers and eventually the missionaries who brought Christianity, reading and writing.

Prior to European arrival, Maori had no distance weapons except for spears, and the introduction of the musket had a significant impact on Maori warfare. Tribes with muskets attacked tribes without any so goods were soon traded with the Europeans for guns.

As more European settlers arrived and France showed interest in taking control of the islands, the British government wanted to gain full control of New Zealand.

In 1840 more than 500 Maori chiefs signed the Treaty of Waitangi, giving power of government to Britain in return for the rights of British citizens as well as guaranteed possession of their lands and other 'treasures'.

Post—treaty, Maori had their land confiscated or bought, leading to the New Zealand Land Wars between Maori and colonial forces which broke out in the 1860s. With the British forcibly taking land from Maori, along with disease, disillusionment, assimilation and alcohol abuse, the population decreased significantly by the end of the 19th century.

The population later began to rise again and the issues facing Maori in the North Island were not the same as those in the more peaceful South Island. This was due to the smaller population of Maori there and the gold rush which made Dunedin the richest city of the South.

With the invention of refrigerated shipping in the 1880s, New Zealand's chief export to Britain changed from wool to frozen meat and dairy products, which significantly boosted the country's economy. Railways were built, new towns were established or expanded and the

Tunisia, May 1943. A group of Maori soldiers eating a meal of "bully" (corned beef) on the Tunis plains just before going into battle. Note the camouflaged vehicle beside them.
AWM/MEC0107

26 .— —. —.. .—— .. —.. ——— .—— ...

Cutella, Italy. April 1944. Warrant Officer (WO) A. Rogers of Central Otagio, NZ, paints a Maori symbol on the side of the Curtiss P40 Kittyhawk aircraft.
AWM/MEC1348

Flying with one of the British rocket Typhoon wings in Normandy, giving close support to the Allied armies in the battle of France, is Flying Officer Mate Alexander Milich, better known as 'Tim,' a Maori from Katai, NZ.
AWM/SUK12846

government helped thousands of British people to start a new life in New Zealand.

By the start of World War I, the country joined Britain to fight against Germany. Three thousand Maori and Pacific islander soldiers served with the New Zealand Army in Gallipoli and on the Western Front as part of the New Zealand (Maori) Pioneer Battalion.

After WWI, Maori culture enjoyed a renaissance due in part to Maori politician Sir Apirana Ngata. At the outbreak of World War II New Zealand contributed around 120,000 troops including the 28th Maori Battalion.

"Where Britain goes, we go! Where she stands, we stand!" announced Michael Savage, the Prime Minister of New Zealand on 3 September 1939 when he formally announced that New Zealand had declared war on Germany.

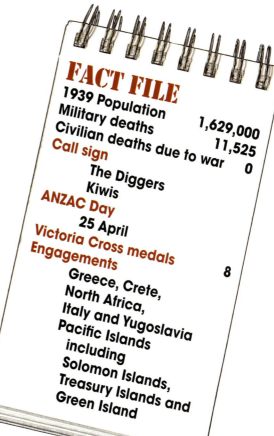

FACT FILE
1939 Population — 1,629,000
Military deaths — 11,525
Civilian deaths due to war — 0
Call sign — The Diggers, Kiwis
ANZAC Day — 25 April
Victoria Cross medals — 8
Engagements — Greece, Crete, North Africa, Italy and Yugoslavia Pacific Islands including Solomon Islands, Treasury Islands and Green Island

Pakeha is the name given by Maori to the European settlers. It means foreign or different.

A fern or koru *and a koru inspired design*

Project: for your eyes only

COVER STORY. You are an artist. Design a logo for the 28th (Maori) Battalion which will be put on badges and worn on uniforms.

Create it in the Maori Koru style.
The koru is the Maori name for a young, unfurling fern frond and symbolizes new life, growth, strength and peace. It is an integral symbol in Maori carving and tattoos.

New Zealand 27

SPECIAL UNIT

The 28th (Maori) Battalion

The battalion was part of the second New Zealand Expeditionary Force (2NZEF) during WWII. The battalion was open to all those of Maori heritage who wanted to join. However, Maori were able to join other battalions too, if they so wished.

Sir Apirana Ngata, along with two Maori MPs, had tried to set up a Maori military unit months before the declaration of war on 3rd September 1939. They were supported by many Maori organisations and the Maori community.

On 4th October 1939, the New Zealand government agreed to set up an infantry battalion of Maori soldiers, but said Maori 'would not be allowed to take up senior roles.'

Maori people agreed to answer to a Pakeha commander but many of them thought it was unfair to have only Pakeha NCOs and commanders (see p13). They believed that their people had enough experience both in European and Maori style military warfare from the Maori Pioneer Battalion days, during World War I as well as in the New Zealand Land Wars to take on senior roles.

While the government refused to change its mind, the Director of Mobilisation selected Major G Dittmer MBE, MC, NZSC as the commanding officer of the battalion and his second-in-command was Lieutenant-Colonel G F Bertrand, who was of mixed European and Maori descent. Both had served overseas in World War I.

Major Dittmer arranged for his army officers to recruit both Pakeha and Maori for selection as commissioned and non-commissioned officers, providing they were medically fit, willing and able. At the end of training, twenty men were recommended for commissions and six were included in the final draft.

The 28th (Maori) Battalion was declared on active service on 13 March 1940 and left on 1 May 1940 from Aotea Quay in Wellington on the troopship *Aquitania*.

Strengths of new recruits in the 28th Battalion

- *Maori were naturally strong and knew how to use weapons as they had lots of experience using patu and taiaha.*

- *Polynesian culture is one of carefree cheerfulness and optimism which is essential during the perils of war.*

- *While in training, Maori were already used to sharing and living close to each other, unlike Pakeha men. New recruits had no problems adjusting to army life.*

- *Maori had a history of fighting between their own tribes as well as against common enemies. This meant that they knew how to join together and fight.*

Weaknesses of new recruits in the 28th Battalion

- *Maori were generally only used to working on farms and all specialists such as medical orderlies, mechanics, clerks, drivers, radio technicians, signallers had to be trained from scratch.*

- *Medically Maori men had bad teeth and also often complained of sore feet, as Maori feet were wider than the issued Pakeha boots.*

- *The men often performed duties for each other and borrowed each other's equipment and clothing. This is not allowed in the army. Soldiers are responsible for their own kit and ensuring that their own duties are carried out. The men often wondered what all the fuss was about. They thought that as long as a rifle and kit were being used by someone, it didn't matter if it wasn't the person to whom it was originally assigned.*

Haka style posturing.
AWM/0077423/376

HAKA

A *haka* is a traditional dance performed by the Maori. It features postures, facial gestures and chants and is performed by a group.

There are many types of haka for different occasions: before battle, to welcome special guests, or just for fun and they are performed by both men and women.

According to Maori folklore, the *haka* was derived from Tanerore, son of the sun god Ra and Hine-raumati the essence of summer who performed the *wiriwiri* or trembling shimmer that you see today in the trembling of the *haka* performer's hands.

The New Zealand *All Blacks* and *Black Ferns* rugby teams, before the start of each match, perform a *haka*. It was first performed in 1888 by the New Zealand Native Team on their first overseas tour of England. The *haka*, still performed to this day, is called the *Ka mate!* It is a pre-battle challenge, which stirs the crowd into a frenzy and unnerves their opponents.

The *Ka mate! haka* was created by Maori chief Te Rauparaha and it tells the story of his pursuit and escape from members of opposing tribes, his fear of being captured and the thrill of his ultimate survival.

Members of the Maori Battalion who had fought in Greece perform a haka *for the King of Greece at Helwan, Egypt in June 1941.*
ATL/DA01229-F

Ka mate! Ka mate!
Tis death! Tis death!
Ka ora! Ka ora!
Tis life! Tis life
Ka mate! Ka mate!
Tis death! Tis death!
Ka ora! Ka ora!
Tis life! Tis life!
Tenei te pangata puhuruhuru
Behold! There stands the hairy man!
Nana nei i tiki mai, whakawhiti te ra !
Who will cause the sun to shine!
A, hupane! A, kaupane!
One step upwards…
A, hupane! A, kaupane!
Another step upwards
Whiti te ra
The sun shines!

Haka peruperu war dance

In Maori culture, warriors, fighting with stone and wooden patus, taiahas and taos, were admired. Fighting was always at close range as they had no long distance weapons. Facial expressions and contortions are an important part of a *haka*, particularly to show menace and aggression. Movements such as dilation of the eyes and staring intensely while distorting the face, emphasise the meaning of the words.

Pukana	rolling back the eyes to show only the whites
Whetero	sticking out the tongue
Whakapi	contorting the body and features
Weru	projecting or protruding the lips
Tahu	staring wildly and distorting the face
Potete	a grimace
Patu	club
Taiaha	fighting staff
Tao	spear

Project: For your eyes only

 COVER STORY. You are an Officer in the Maori Battalion. Your troops are tired and you need to motivate them.

Create a chant to go with a *haka* to boost their spirits.

New Zealand 29

28th (Maori) Battalion Marching Song

In the days that have now gone
when the Maoris went to war
They fought and fought until the last
man died for the honour of their tribe
And so we carry on
the conditions they have laid
And as we go on day by day
You will always hear us say...

Maori Battalion march to victory
Maori Battalion staunch and true
Maori Battalion march to glory
Take the honour of the people
with you
We will march, march, march to
the enemy
And we'll fight right to the end.
For God! For King! And for Country!
AU - E! Ake, ake, kia kaha e!

A loyal band of Maoris
Sailing from New Zealand
To win us freedom and peace
Marching shoulder to shoulder onward
And we will shout again
Ake aka kia kaha e
Haere tonu haere tonu ra
Kia - o - ra Kia - o – ra

This marching song was written in 1939 by Corporal Anania Amohau of the Te Arawa people. It became one of the most popular songs sung by New Zealand soldiers during World War II.

28th (Maori) Battalion

There were four Companies of the Maori Battalion, which were organised on tribal lines:

- **A Company** was comprised of men from Ngapuhi, Te Aupouri and other Tai Tokerau peoples. Callsign GUMDIGGERS
- **B Company** was drawn from the Te Arawa, Tuhoe and Tuwharetoa peoples from Rotorua, the Bay of Plenty, Taupo and the Coromandel area. Callsign PENNY DIVERS
- **C Company** was made up of the Ngati Porou and Rongowhakaata peoples from the East Cape to the south of Gisborne. Callsign COWBOYS
- **D Company** contained all others from Waikato/Maniapoto, Taranaki, Kahungunu and Te Waipounamu peoples. Callsign NGATI WALKABOUT

Members of the 28th (Maori) Battalion on board HMT Batory. AWM/004333

HONOURS AND AWARDS FO

Victoria Cross (VC)
Moana Nui a Kiwa Ngarimu

Distinguished Service Order (DSO)
Lt-Col A. Awatere, MC,
Lt-Col F. Baker,
Lt-Col C.M. Bennet,
Lt-Col G. Dittmer, MBE, MC,
Lt-Col R.R.T. Young,
Maj J.C. Henare,
Lt M. Wikiriwhi

Member of the Order of the British Empire (MBE)
Mr C.B. Bennet
 (YMCA, attached)

Bar to Military Cross
Capt J.S. Baker, MC
Capt W. Porter, MC
Capt R. Royal

Military Cross
Maj W.S.L. Mcrae
Maj H.W. Northcroft
Maj W. Reedy
Capt A. Awatere
Capt C.N. D'Arcy
 (NZMC, attached)
Capt I.G. Harris
Capt K.A. Keiha
Capt H.C.A. Lambert
Capt J. Matehaere
Capt P.F.TeH. Ornberg
Capt R. Royal
Capt Te M.R. Tomoana
Capt M. Wikiriwhi, DSO
Lt W. Porter
Lt Te R.W. Tibble
Lt J.P. Tikao-Barrett

Project: For your eyes only

COVER STORY.
You are a new recruit of the 28th (Maori) Battalion. You are training to be a signaller. Write a diary describing the training, the problems that you and your fellow privates face and how you feel about leaving for the War in Europe. You have never travelled on a boat before and prior to enlisting you were a farm worker.

How do your family and tribal chief feel about you fighting for New Zealand in a foreign land?

"While the 28th (Maori) Battalion won and continues to be rightly celebrated as a unique and most effective Battalion with a distinct identity, it was only 20% of the total Maori contribution to WWII. Maori served throughout other battalions of the 2nd New Zealand Expeditionary Force, the Royal New Zealand Navy and the Royal New Zealand Air Force."

*Dr Stephen Clarke
Chief Executive
Royal New Zealand
Returned and Services'
Association*

ERVICE DURING WORLD WAR II

2 Lt J.S. Baker
2 Lt B.G. Christy
2 Lt A. Huata
2 Lt P.O. Lambly
Rev W. Te T. Huata
  (Chaplain, attached)

Distinguished Conduct Medal
WO I T Mcrae
WO I A C Wood
Sgt R Davis
Sgt J W Mataira
L-Sgt H Manahi*
Cpl H K Barrett
Cpl P Rakena
Cpl W Teneti
Cpl N Tuakti
Pte T Heka
Pte L Helmbright
Pte P Maangi
Pte C Shelford

*****Lance Sergeant Haane Manahi**: *a claim was lodged in 2000 that Manahi should be posthumously awarded the VC for bravery at the Battle of Takrouna, North Africa.*

An allied attack on Takrouna Ridge in North Africa had failed but early on 20 April 1943 two platoons of Maori soldiers, one led by Sgt Manahi and the other by Sgt Johnny Rogers, attacked from the back of the hill in different directions. They fought their way up a steep limestone escarpment under heavy Italian and German fire. The battle was then won by Sgt Manahi and his fellow Maori soldiers. Corps Commander Lieutenant-General Sir Brian Horrocks had observed most of the action and said of Manahi that it was the bravest act he had witnessed during the War.

At the time, four generals had recommended that Manahi receive the VC but the recommendation was downgraded to a Distinguished Conduct Medal (see left). Queen Elizabeth II was unable to award him a VC as her father, King George VI, said that no more awards for WWII bravery could be given and she did not want to go against her father's wishes.

However Queen Elizabeth II recognised Manahi's courage with the gift of a letter, a sword and an altar cloth inspired by the famous refrain 'For God, For King, And for Country!' from the Marching Song of the 28th (Maori) Battalion. (see left). The Queen's son, Prince Andrew, presented those gifts to Manahi's son at a special ceremony in Rotorua in March 2007.

New Zealand

PEOPLE PROFILES Nancy Grace Augusta Wake AC, GM (the White Mouse)

The most decorated female servicewoman in WWII

AWM/PO1685.001

FACT FILE
Code names
The White Mouse, Heléne, Madame Andrée, Witch
D.O.B 30 August 1912
P.O.B Wellington, New Zealand
Service/Branch
   Special Operations Executive (SOE), First Aid Nursing Yeomanry (FANY)
Years of service 1943—1945
Rank Captain
Unit Freelance
Engagements
   World War II behind enemy lines in France
Awards
   Companion of the Order of Australia
   George Medal
   Chevalier de la Légion d'Honneur (France)
   Croix de Guerre (France)
   Medal of Freedom (USA)
   RSA Badge in Gold (NZ)
Other Work
   Nurse
   Intelligence Officer
   Politician

Nancy Wake was born in New Zealand in 1912 Like many European settler families she came from a genetic melting pot. Her family's origins were French Huguenot, English and Maori.

When she was a small child, her family moved to Sydney, Australia, and at 16 she ran away from home to train as a nurse. An aunt died and left her £200, and she used this money to travel the world, finally training as a journalist in London. By 1935 she was reporting from Europe and witnessed first-hand the violent protests against the Jews and gypsies by the Nazis.

Having now married French industrialist Henri Fiocca, she was living in Marseilles when France was invaded by the Germans in 1939. Nancy joined the French Resistance and worked as a courier. She was perceived as a massive threat by the Germans, who tapped her telephone, intercepted her mail and gave her the code name 'White Mouse.'

Her life was in constant danger, and by 1943 she was the Gestapo's most wanted person. They offered five million francs to anyone who could hand her over. By year end, Nancy had to flee Marseilles, leaving her husband behind; he was later captured, tortured and killed by the Germans. He had refused to give any information about his wife to his captors and he died because of it.

After several dangerous attempts to cross the Pyrenees mountains into Spain, Nancy finally made it and travelled to Britain to join the SOE.

She became one of 39 women and 430 men in the French Section of the SOE whose job was to work with French resistance groups and to find ways to stop the Germans. Her training with SOE included survival skills, silent killing, codes, radio operation and night parachuting. She often had to work with plastic explosives, Sten guns, rifles, pistols and grenades. Her official cover story was that she was part of the First Aid Nursing Yeomanry.

In April 1944 Nancy Wake parachuted into Auvergne where she remained until the liberation of France.

She was the liaison between London and the local *Maquis* resistance group. Always brave with a proud fighting spirit, she coordinated resistance activity, recruited

SPECIAL UNIT

> Nancy Wake's great grandmother, Pourewa, was the first Maori to marry a white man, in 1836.

SPECIAL OPERATIONS EXECUTIVE (SOE)

Code Names:
- Baker Street Irregulars
- Churchill's Secret Army
- The Ministry of Ungentlemanly Warfare

SOE was established by British Prime Minister Winston Churchill and Minister of Economic Warfare Hugh Dalton in July 1940 to conduct warfare by means other than direct fighting.

As a British resistance movement, its mission was to place spies behind enemy lines.

A variety of people from all backgrounds, ethnicities and social classes served in the movement. Indeed SOE turned a blind eye to those who were known homosexuals, had criminal records or bad (military) conduct records, were Communist or were even anti-British.

The key attributes for agents were a thorough knowledge of the language and the country in which they had to operate. The SOE was officially dissolved after the War in January 1946.

---

more members and also led attacks on German operations. ==She even killed an SS Sentry with her bare hands to stop him from raising the alarm.==

One of her crowning achievements came when Nancy cycled 500km in just 71 hours through several German checkpoints to replace codes that her wireless operator had been forced to destroy during a German raid. Without the codes they could not order supplies or weapon drops. She made the journey almost non-stop through mountains and countryside. After the War her achievements were formally recognised with medals and awards.

Nancy Wake received the George Medal from Britain for leadership and bravery under fire, the US Medal of Freedom, the *Médaille de la Résistance* and the *Croix de Guerre* with two bronze palms and a silver star from France.

She wrote her autobiography in 1988 entitled '*The White Mouse.*' After working for the Intelligence Department for the British Air Ministry, she returned to Australia in 1960 and stood as a Liberal political candidate. In 1988 she received the French title of Chevalier of the Legion of Honour.

In 2004 she was made a Companion of the Order of Australia and in 2006 she was awarded the Royal New Zealand Returned and Services Association's highest honour – the RSA Badge in Gold. She now she lives in a nursing home for veterans in London.

Project: For your eyes only

Wake was one of 39 women and 430 men in the French section of the SOE.
Her heritage is a mixture of English, French and Maori.
Do you think she may have experienced any prejudice or discrimination in her life or wartime service? Do you think her appearance would have helped or hindered her work as a secret agent?

Unit 2 New Zealand

PEOPLE PROFILES Second Lieutenant Moana-nui-a-Kiwa Ngarimu VC

Ngarimu VC
used with kind permission from the Kippenberger Military Archive, National Army Museum, NZ. DA11264

FACT FILE
First Maori awarded the VC in World War II
- **D.O.B** 7 April 1919
- **P.O.B** Whareponga, New Zealand
- **D.O.D** 27 March 1943, Tunisia
- **Rank** Second lieutenant
- **Unit** 2nd New Zealand Expeditionary Force 28th (Maori) Battalion
- **Engagements** World War II, North Africa Campaign
- **Awards** Victoria Cross
- **Other work** Farm work

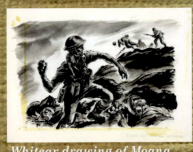

Whitear drawing of Moana
NA/INF-3-471

When the war broke out, Ngarimu enlisted in the 28th (Maori) Battalion and sailed with the Second Echelon of the Second New Zealand Expeditionary Force.

He was commissioned on ANZAC Day 1942, and served as an intelligence officer until he was called upon to command a platoon of C Company (Ngati Porou) of the Maori Battalion.

Second Lieutenant Ngarimu was killed in action at Tebaga Gap, Tunisia on 27 March 1943, and is buried at the Sfax War Cemetery, Tunisia.

He was awarded a VC posthumously and the citation was published in *The London Gazette* on 1 June 1943.

The medal was presented to his parents by Governor General Sir Cyril Newall at a Hui in Ruatoria on 6 October 1943. It is now held at the Tairawhiti Museum, Gisborne, New Zealand.

An accomplished sportsman, Ngarimu represented the East Coast in rugby in 1937.

Ngarimu's father was a chief of the Ngati Porou and his mother's people were from the Whanau-a-Apanui tribe.

NA/ZJ973-2559

Project: For your eyes only

COVER STORY.
You are a member of the platoon who fought alongside Second Lieutenant Moana-nui-a-Kiwa Ngarimu at Tebaga Gap.

Write a letter to his parents describing the bravery of his actions and how sad the platoon is that he died.

34

PEOPLE PROFILES
Captain Kingi Areta Keiha

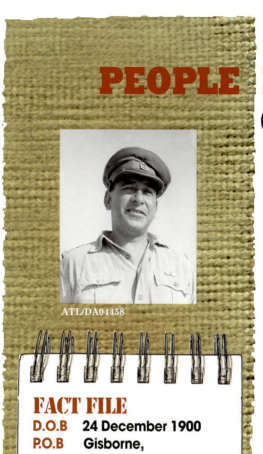
ATL/DA04458

FACT FILE
D.O.B 24 December 1900
P.O.B Gisborne, New Zealand
D.O.D 29 May 1961, New Zealand
Years of Service
  1940—1944
Rank Captain
Engagements
  World War II
    Battle of Greece
    Battle of Crete
    North Africa Campaign
Awards
  Military Cross
Other work
  Law clerk
  Interpreter
  Maori welfare officer
  Farmer

Kingi Areta Keiha was principally from the Rongowhakaata, Te Aitanga-a-Mahaki and Te Aitanga-a-Hauiti tribes.

His first job was as a law clerk in 1920 and later he worked as an interpreter of Maori and English.

At the start of WWII, Keiha enlisted as a member of the original 28th (Maori) Battalion, which was declared on active service in March 1940. He held the rank of second lieutenant in C Company.

Keiha and the Battalion fought in Greece, Crete and then North Africa. For his action during the battles at El Alamein he was awarded the Military Cross for gallantry.

Keiha was part of a counter-attack against Field Marshal Erwin Rommel's attempt to reach Cairo and Alexandria. The award citation stated he 'prepared for his difficult task well and executed it excellently'.

When Lieutenant Colonel CM Bennett was wounded at Takrouna, Keiha commanded the battalion from 22 April to 11 September 1943. Command was later passed on to Lieutenant Colonel MC Fairbrother when Keiha was evacuated to hospital.

In November 1943 Keiha returned to New Zealand and there he arranged for the eventual return home of the battalion. He also assisted with establishing the Maori Rehabilitation Head office in Wellington and become a Maori rehabilitation officer.

In the early 1950s he was appointed Tairawhiti district Maori welfare officer at Gisborne. A dedicated public servant, he was a trustee and member of Te Hokowhitu-a-Tu Maori Veterans' Association and a member of the Maori Soldiers' Trust Committee. In 1958 he was elected president of the Gisborne branch of the 28th New Zealand (Maori) Battalion Association and a member of the Gisborne Returned Services Association Executive.

Captain K A Keiha died in 1961. He was survived by his wife and four children. A memorial headstone was unveiled by Brigadier George Dittmer who was the battalion's first commanding officer from the New Zealand 28th (Maori) Battalion Association at Keiha's burial plot.

New Zealand 35

SECTION 1 AUSTRALASIA

Unit 3: Pacific Islands

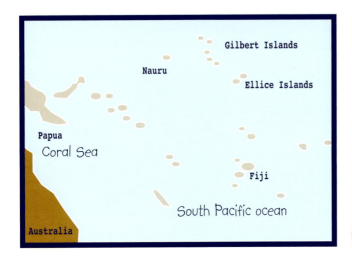

There are between 20,000 and 30,000 islands in the Pacific Ocean. Those which lie to the south of the Tropic of Cancer, not including Australia, are grouped in three divisions called Melanesia, Micronesia and Polynesia. The people who live here are called Pacific Islanders.

During the War, the Japanese invaded and occupied some of these islands including the British Solomon Islands and Bougainville in the Territory of New Guinea. Here they built naval and air bases in an attempt to interrupt supply lines between the USA, Australia and New Zealand.

The Allies fought back by land, air and sea and did serious damage to Japanese military equipment and supplies.

The British colonies of Fiji and the Solomon Islands were very important to the Allies and special units of local men were raised to help protect them.

Fiji's strategic position made it one of the best locations in the Pacific for the Allies, including the Fiji Infantry Regiment, to fight against the Japanese army. New Zealand and USA troops used Fiji as a training and resupply base. By July 1942 there were about 40,000 American, New Zealand and Fiji troops defending Fiji.

Canoes, Coconuts And A Future President

The coconut shell on President Kennedy's desk at the White House in August 1962.
KNC 23153

On 2 August 1943 an American patrol torpedo boat known as PT-109 collided with a Japanese destroyer and sank.

The crew escaped and swam to an islet three-and-a-half miles away led by their commanding officer, the future US President, Lieutenant John F Kennedy.

Biuku Gasa and Eroni Kumana were coastwatchers from the Solomon Islands. They were ordered to look for survivors and patrolled the area in their dugout canoes. They found the crew, had been living on coconuts, six days later. However, there were two problems which prevented Gasa and Kumana from rescuing the stranded Americans. One was that their small dugout canoes couldn't carry the surviving 11 men. The other was that the rescuers couldn't speak English. So Gasa gave Kennedy a coconut husk and indicated that he write a message on the inside which he did. The message read:

NAURO ISL COMMANDER . . . NATIVE KNOWS POS'IT . . . HE CAN PILOT . . . 11 ALIVE NEED SMALL BOAT . . . KENNEDY

Gasa and Kumana delivered the message by rowing 35 miles through enemy waters to the nearest Allied base and soon the crew were successfully rescued. Years later Kennedy invited Gasa and Kumana to attend his presidential inauguration but the pair were mistakenly turned back at the airport and officials sent other representatives. The men were finally recognised in 2002 and again in 2007 at a special presentation.

SPECIAL UNITS

The Fiji Infantry Regiment

Name The Fiji Infantry Regiment
Branch Fiji Defence Force, Republic of Fiji Military Forces
Active 1920—Present
Engagements World War II Pacific Campaign
Commanders Colonel J E Workman (New Zealand Defence Force)

At the outbreak of war the regiment's main purpose was to protect vulnerable points such as fuel dumps and important government buildings. Once the Americans joined the war, they took command of the Fiji Defence Force

South Pacific Scouts

Name South Pacific Scouts
Branch 3 Division
Active 1942—1944
Engagements Solomon Islands, New Georgia
Commanders Captain D E Williams

The South Pacific Scouts were a jungle warfare unit formed from Fijians and Solomon Islanders. The soldiers wore camouflaged American jungle suits and New Zealand army boots. They were armed with Owen guns, rifles, revolvers and hand grenades and carried five days' worth of food rations at a time.

South Pacific Scouts. PAColl-4161-01-113-01_mm

The Coastwatchers

Name Coast Watch Organisation, Combined Field Intelligence Service
Code Name Ferdinand
Branch Allied Intelligence Bureau, South West Pacific Area
Active 1942—1945
Engagements World War II Pacific Campaign
Commanders Lieutenant Commander Eric Feldt (Australia)

The Coastwatchers' role was to observe enemy movements and rescue stranded Allied personnel. They were mostly Australian military officers, New Zealand servicemen, Pacific Islanders and escaped Allied prisoners of war.

Feldt named his unit after Ferdinand the bull in a children's story.

"*Ferdinand ... did not fight but sat under a tree and just smelled the flowers. It was meant as a reminder to Coastwatchers that it was not their duty to fight and so draw attention to themselves, but to sit circumspectly and unobtrusively, gathering information.*"

First Infantry Battalion in New Georgia fire a Vickers machine gun in 1944. AWM/305273

Pacific Islands 37

PEOPLE PROFILES Corporal Sefanaia Sukanaivalu vc

The only Fijian to receive the Victoria Cross

FACT FILE
D.O.B 1 January 1918
P.O.B Yacata, Fiji
D.O.D 23 June 1944
Years of service
   Unknown—1944
Rank Corporal
Unit 3rd Battalion Fiji Infantry Regiment
Engagements
   World War II
   Bougainville Campaign
Awards
   Victoria Cross

CITATION

"On June 23rd, 1944 at Mawaraka, Bougainville, in the Solomon Islands, Cpl. Sefanaia Sukanaivalu crawled forward to rescue some men wounded when their platoon was ambushed. After recovering two men this N.C.O. volunteered to go alone through heavy fire to try and rescue another - but on the way back was seriously wounded and fell to the ground unable to move further. Several unsuccessful attempts were made to rescue him; and realising that his men would not withdraw while he was still alive Cpl. Sukanaivalu raised himself up in front of the Japanese machine gun and was riddled with bullets. This brave Fiji soldier, after rescuing two wounded men with the greatest heroism and being gravely wounded himself, deliberately sacrificed his own life knowing that in no other way could his men be induced to retire from a situation in which they must have been annihilated."

The London Gazette, 2 November 1944

Corporal Sukanaivalu is buried at Bitapaka War Graves Commission Cemetery, in Papua New Guinea. Sukanaivalu's heroic tale was featured in America's prestigious *Time* magazine on Christmas Day 1944.

Project: For your eyes only

Cover Story.
You are a reporter.

Write an article about the heroic Pacific Islanders for *Time* magazine and illustrate it with photographs or drawings. Add comments from American marines and survivors who served alongside the Islanders.

Troops of the Fiji Infantry Regiment preparing for overseas service against the Japanese in the Solomon Islands.
IWM/K6932

PEOPLE PROFILES

Sir Jacob Charles Vouza GM, OBE

The most highly decorated Solomon Islander Scout

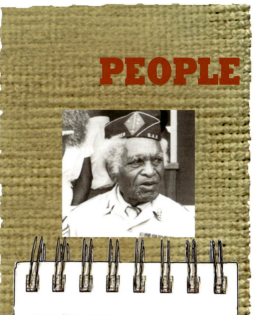

FACT FILE
D.O.B 1900
P.O.B Koli, Guadalcanal, Solomon Islands
D.O.D 15 March 1984
Years of service
   1916—1941 Constabulary
   1942 - 1945 Coastwatchers
Rank Sergeant Major (Constabulary)
Unit Coastwatchers
Engagements
   World War II
Awards
   Silver Star (USA)
   Legion of Merit (USA)
   George Medal (UK)
   Police Long Service Medal
   Member of Order of the British Empire (OBE)
   Knight Bachelor
Other Work
   Police Officer
   President of Guadalcanal Council
   British Solomon Islands Protectorate Advisory Council Member

Vouza had been a police sergeant major who served for 25 years before retiring in 1941.

However, when the Japanese invaded the Solomon Islands, he returned to active service and in 1942 he joined the Coastwatchers. In August that year, Vouza rescued a downed US naval pilot and guided him to friendly lines where he met the US Marines for the first time. After this meeting, Vouza volunteered to become a scout for the Americans behind enemy lines.

A few weeks later, while on a scouting mission to locate enemy lookout stations, Vouza was captured by the Japanese. They found he was carrying a small American flag so they tied him to a tree and tried to force him to reveal information about the Allies. He was questioned and tortured for hours but he refused to talk. The Japanese then left him in the jungle to die.

Vouza chewed through the vines that restrained him and crawled for three miles through the jungle to reach the American camp. Before accepting medical treatment, he reported everything that he had seen. The Americans said that this information led to an Allied victory at the subsequent Battle of the Tenaru in Guadalcanal. After 12 days in hospital where he received 16 pints of blood, Vouza returned to duty as the chief scout for the Marines.

Vouza received a number of awards including the American Silver Star and Legion of Merit for refusing to give information under Japanese torture and for outstanding service.

The British awarded him the George Medal for gallant conduct and exceptional devotion to duty. In 1957 he received an OBE, and in 1979 he was knighted for his long and faithful government service. Sir Jacob Vouza died in 1984.

In 2002 a postage stamp was designed in his honour to celebrate the 60th Anniversary of the Battle of Guadalcanal in August 1942.

Pacific Islands 39

SECTION 2 INDIA and the FAR EAST

Unit 1: India

This unit will explore the role that India, known at the time as the 'Jewel in the Crown' of the British Empire, played in World War II.

India has an interesting and complex history and culture which goes back almost six thousand years. The earliest known civilisation started in the Indus Valley, now modern-day Pakistan. Between 3250 and 1500BC, the Aryans came from the north and moved across the country, spreading their culture and the Hindu religion.

In 567BC, Gautama Buddha, the founder of Buddhism, was born. At about the same time a man called Mahavira started the Jain religion. In the 4th century BC, Emperor Ashoka, one of the greatest leaders in India's history, led the Mauryan Empire which ruled over most of the country.

Following their reign the Guptas governed the north, while the south was controlled by the Hindu empires of the Cholas, the Pandyas and the Cheras. These empires grew and traded with Europe and Asia until the 12th century.

Meanwhile Jews and Christians arrived in the years following the death of Christ. In about the 7th century the Zoroastrians (Parsis) settled in Gujarat and added their beliefs to the mix of religions that is present in India today.

The 12th century saw the introduction of Islam by Muhammad of Goran, an Afghan ruler who conquered parts of northern India including Delhi. His sultanate was attacked and weakened in 1398 by 'Timur the Lame' from Turkey, leaving the way open for the Mughals from Iran to take control of the north.

In southern India during the 14th century, the Hindu Vijayanagar Empire was put in place.

In the 15th century, the Sikh religion was established in the Punjab region of northern India.

By the early 1600s, the Portuguese, French, Dutch, Danish and British started to arrive and gain control of different territories. But it was the British who

Mahatma Gandhi was an Indian civil rights leader who led the Quit India *campaign which called for independence from Great Britain. He and his followers protested using non-violent ways such as hunger strikes and civil disobedience, which eventually succeeded. Unfortunately he was assassinated six months after independence was granted in January 1948.* IWM/IND005083

Indian women training for air raid precautions (ARP) duties in Bombay. IWM/IND1492

A British sister instructs an Indian nurse how to adjust a doctor's mask at a first aid post in Calcutta. IWM/IND1869

eventually took over, firstly through trade and then by direct governance. India became a British colony in 1858. However by 1885 a locally-run political group, the Indian National Congress (INC), was given more responsibility for the running of the country. By the end of World War I, there were strong calls for Great Britain to leave and for India to govern itself.

These calls for independence continued up until the start of World War II. Great Britain was in a difficult position: it required India's resources including manpower, to face the war but didn't want to give away its precious colony. So in 1939 the then British leader in India (called a viceroy,) Lord Linlithgow, formally declared India's entry into the War without asking the INC. This angered many Indians.

World War II was India's biggest and most devastating war. It was also a war in which Indians fought for both the Allied and Axis powers. While the INC was opposed to the totalitarian and racist regimes of the Axis powers, it also felt that it should not fight for the British, who had denied India its own freedom.

At the outbreak of war, the Indian Army had 205,000 men. This later rose to some 2.5million, all of whom were volunteers. It was the largest volunteer contribution of any nation during the War.

Indian troops played a major role in the Middle East and African campaigns, fighting against the Nazis and Italian fascists. They were also the third largest Allied contingent (after the Americans and British) in the liberation of Italy. Crucially they played a key role in defeating the Japanese in Burma.

FACT FILE
1939 Population	378,000,000
Military deaths	87,000
Civilian deaths	1,500,000

Campaigns
- Burma
- Italy
- Western Africa
- East Africa
- North Africa

VC Medals: 28
The Gurkhas were awarded 10 of these medals

Subhash Chandra Bose was vehemently opposed to British rule of India. Bose formed the Indian National Army (INA) and the Provisional Government of Free India which aligned itself with the Axis powers.

The INA grew to a strength of 50,000 men and fought the Allies at Imphal and Burma in 1944. There was even a women's regiment called the Rani of Jhansi Regiment that engaged in active combat in Burma.

However by the end of WWII none of INA's allies had supported its efforts. After the War three INA officers were prosecuted for treason but the trial drew so much public sympathy that Britian's decision to give India its independence followed shortly after. Bose is believed to have died on 18 August 1945 in a plane crash over Taiwan. But his dream of an independent India did eventually come true in 1947.

India 41

INDIAN ARMED FORCES

During WWII, India's weapons included tank, artillery and airborne forces and was the largest all-volunteer movement in history, comprising more than 2.5 million personnel. Around 87,000 lost their lives, an unknown number became prisoners of war and 6,000 were liberated by Allied forces between 1943 and 1945.

Royal Indian Air Force*

The RIAF supported land operations against Imperial Japanese forces in Burma (Myanmar). By August 1945, the IAF had 25,000 personnel of nine squadrons equipped with Spitfire and Hurricane fighters.

*King George VI called it the Royal Indian Air Force in recognition of its services in World War II, but the prefix 'Royal' was removed after India gained independence.

A student Indian RIAF pilot with flying kit photographed beside his Hurricane before a training flight at a Flying Training School at Kohat, in the North West Frontier Province of India. The commanding officer of the station was Wing Commander Mukerjee. IWM/IB1330

A scout car crew of 6th Duke of Connaught's Own Lancers, Indian Armoured Corps, chat with youngsters in San Felice, Italy during the advance towards the River Sangro. IWM/NA008592

British Indian Army Indian Army (IA)

Initially, only British soldiers were permitted to become officers, but later Indian soldiers in the IA were allowed to do so too. Until 1932 officers, both British and Indian, were trained at the Royal Military Academy at Sandhurst in Britian. The IA established the Indian Military Academy in Dehradun and officers were able to receive their training there from 1932.

Fitters of the RAF and Royal Indian Air Force work on the Pratt & Whitney Twin Wasp engine of a Consolidated Catalina at Korangi Creek, near Karachi. IWMCI1457

Flying Officer P C Ramachandran, wearing a flying helmet, smiles from the cockpit of his aircraft, prior to a test flight, somewhere in Britain. Ramachandran was later promoted to an air commodore with the RIAF. IWM/D9503

An elephant pulling a Supermarine Walrus aircraft into position at a Fleet Air Arm station. IWM/A24291

An Indian infantry section of the 2nd Battalion, 7th Rajput Regiment, about to go on patrol on the Arakan front, Burma. IND 2917

An Indian naval rating operating a signal lamp on the sloop Sutlej *at the Royal Indian Naval Station at Calcutta.*
IWM/IB1535

Crew of the Indian sloop Narbada *at Myebon, Burma. The gun barrels were blistered during the bombardment of the Arakan coast.*
IWM/IND4387

Trainee mechanical engineers at work in the Royal Indian Navy's shore establishment, HMIS Talwar *near Bombay.* IWM/IND43

A look-out on board a Royal Indian Navy sloop scans the horizon using binoculars during anti-submarine escort duties in the Indian Ocean, 1945.
IWM/IND4218

Royal Indian Navy* (RIN)

During the war the RIN fleet consisted of:

4 x 1200 ton Erget
2 x 1470 ton Black Swan
4 x 1460 ton River class
4 x 925 ton Flower class corvettes
9 x 650 ton Minesweepers
6 Sloops

The RIN successfully sunk two enemy submarines, but lost two sloops: *HMIS Pathan* and *HMIS Indus*.

*When India became a republic in 1950, the 'Royal' prefix was dropped. The prefix had been added in 1892 when the fleet was known as the Royal Indian Marine.

Project: For your eyes only

COVER STORY. Operation Join Now
You are a recruiting officer for the Indian Armed Forces. Design an advertising campaign to recruit Indians into the Army, Navy or Air Force. What would be the best way to reach them? Would you use newspapers, radio, cinema, posters or other media? Design posters, radio and cinema ads, write a newspaper article. How else could you reach them?

Chief Officer Margaret L Cooper, Deputy Director of the Women's Royal Indian Naval Service (WRINS), with Second Officer Kalyani Sen. They wear 'Straight RN' gold rings in place of the usual WRNS blue and the Chief Officer wears a naval officer's cap badge, rather than the blue of British WRNS officers. IWM/A029070

Women in the Armed Forces

Both European and Indian women played a significant role in India's Armed Forces. The Women's Auxiliary Corps India was formed in 1942 and was the Indian equivalent of the ATS (see page 92). They served in support roles for all three forces, army, navy and air force.

The Women's Royal Indian Naval Service (WRINS) was formed in 1944 and managed the administration of RIN shore establishments.

Women from the Naval Wing of the Women's Auxiliary Corps (India), 1945. IWM/IND4410

India 43

SPECIAL UNITS

Field Marshal Sir William Slim, 14th Army commander, chatting with a Gurkha rifleman in Burma.
IWM/INDSE2952

When you go home don't worry about what to tell your loved ones and friends about service in Asia. No one will know where you were, or where it is if you do. You are, and will remain 'The Forgotten Army.'

Attributed to Field Marshal Sir William Slim. At the time many of the operations of the 14th Army were overlooked or unknown by the European and American newspapers and media.

Formation badge for 14th Army designed by Field Marshal Sir William Slim. Red and black were the colours of the British and Indian Armies. The hilt on the sword forms the 'S', for his own name. On the grip, in Morse code, is the army's title. The sword points downwards to represent the army recapturing Burma from the North.

The Burmese dragon, Chinthe, was the mascot on the formation badge.

The Chindits

The word 'Chindit' comes from the Burmese mythical beast Chinthe, statues of which guard Buddhist temples. Its usage was suggested by Captain Aung Thin DSO of the Burma Rifles.

Name: 77th Indian Infantry Brigade (1943)
Special Force, 3rd (Chindits) Indian Infantry Division (1944)
Branch: IndiaN Army
Call sign: The Chindits
Active: 1942—1945
Engagements: Burma Campaign
Commanders: Major General Orde Wingate DSO
Lieutenant General WDA Lentaigne
VC medals: 4

The Chindits were a special force of long-range penetration troops trained to operate deep behind enemy lines. They consisted of personnel from the British Army, Gurkhas, British Indian Army, Burma Rifles and the Royal West African Frontier Force. The Chindits are regarded as the first of the British and Commonwealth forces to get the better of the Japanese.

The 14th Army

Name: The British Fourteenth Army
Branch: British Army, British Indian Army
Call sign: The Forgotten Army
Active: 1943—1945
Engagements: Burma Campaign
Commander: Field Marshal Sir William Slim

The 14th Army was a Commonwealth force consisting of units from the Indian Army, British Army, and West and East African divisions within the British Army.

By 1945, not only was it the largest army in the Commonwealth, but, it was also the largest single army in the world.

The troops of 14th Army, closing in on Mandalay walk over ground littered with the bodies and equipment of the Japanese in February 1945.
IWMSE3114

> "Bravest of the brave, most generous of the generous, never had a country more faithful friends than you."
>
> Sir Ralph Turner MC, a British professor at the School of Oriental Studies who served wih the 2nd/3rd Queen Alexandre's Own Gurkha Rifles, who was himself awarded a Military Cross, said this about the Gurkhas.

Above: Netrabahadur Thapa of the 5th Royal Gurkha Rifles, posthumously awarded the Victoria Cross. IWM/IND3956
Left: Two Gurkhas with their Kukries. AWM/129263

The Gurkhas

Name:	The Gurkhas
Branch:	British Indian Army, British Army
Active:	1817—Present
Engagements:	Burma Campaign
	Syria
	North Africa
	Italy
	Greece
	India
	Singapore

Gurkha motto: "Better to die than be a coward."
The Gurkha war cry:
'Jai Mahakali, Ayo Gorkhali' which literally translates to "Glory be to the Goddess of War, here come the Gurkhas!"

The Gurkhas are famous for their bravery and strength and are an important part of the British Empire's military history. Originating from Nepal, these warriors impressed the early 19th century Britons whom they initially fought against. The British soon hired Gurkhas as mercenaries after reaching a stalemate during the Gurkha Wars of 1814-1816. The British granted Nepal protectorate status and Gurkha regiments were formed within the British Indian Army.

The Gurkhas are dominated by four ethnic groups: the **Gurung** and **Magar** from central Nepal and the **Rai** and **Limbu** from the east. The name Gurkha, sometimes spelt as 'Gorkha' or 'Ghurka,' is taken from the 8th century Hindu Warrior-Saint Guru Gorakhnath. Legend tells that he gave his loyal disciple, Bappa Rawal, the Kukri, or curved knife which is still used to this day. A quarter of a million Gurkhas served during WWII, earning nearly 3,000 bravery awards including 10 VC medals. The Gurkhas suffered 32,000 casualties.

GURKHA VICTORIA CROSS WINNERS

Lalbahadur Thapa	Agansing Rai
Bhanbhagta Gurung	Gaje Ghale
Lachiman Gurung	Netrabahadur Thapa*
Sher Thapa*	Thaman Gurung*
Tulbahadur Pun	Ganju Lama

Awarded the Victoria Cross posthumously

Did you know...
HRH Prince Harry served with a Gurkha battalion during his tour of duty in Afghanistan.

Project: For your eyes only

 You are a journalist. Write a newspaper article or television interview about either the 14th Army, the Chindits or the Gurkhas.

 In 2009 there was a controversy about the Gurkhas veterans who wanted to retire in Great Britain. Write an article or debate the issue in class.

India 45

PEOPLE PROFILE
Jemadar Nand Singh VC, MVC
India's most highly decorated soldier

Nand Singh was a member of the the Sikh Regiment which received the most medals of any regiment in the British Empire.

He was awarded the VC for his incredible actions against the Japanese on 11—12 March 1944 in Arakan in Burma.

The Japanese held a position called India Hill, which had a very steep, knife-edged ridge. Singh and his platoon were ordered to capture this position. As Singh and his men approached, they were met with heavy machine-gun and rifle fire which killed or injured most of them.

Singh moved forward alone, even though he was injured. He then captured the first trench and killed the two Japanese occupants with his bayonet.

Following this, he moved on to the second and third trenches, again sustaining injuries from the continuous heavy fire and grenades of the Japanese. Again he silenced them with his bayonet – single-handedly.

What he achieved took a matter of minutes. When his platoon reached him, they captured the position using bayonets and grenades to kill 37 of the 40 Japanese who had held the position.

Singh was wounded six times, but showed incredible bravery, determination, and a total disregard for his own life or safety. He was awarded with Great Britain's highest honour—the Victoria Cross.

Following India's independence, Singh remained in the Indian Army and fought in the Indo-Pakistani War.

A Sikh regiment clears a Japanese foxhole with machine-gun fire after throwing in a phosphorus grenade.
IWM/IND4550

On 12 December 1947 he led his platoon of D Company to rescue his battalion from an ambush in Uri, Kashmir. During the battle Singh was killed by machine-gun fire at close range.

IWM/IND3975

FACT FILE:
- **D.O.B.** 24 September 1914
- **P.O.B** Bhatinda, Punjab India
- **D.O.D** 12 December 1947 Uri, Kashmir
- **Years of service** 1933—1947
- **Rank** Jemadar (Viceroy's Commissioned Officer (VCO)
- **Unit** 1/11th Sikh Regiment
- **Engagements** Burma Campaign Indo-Pakistan War
- **Awards** Victoria Cross (VC) Maha Vir Chakra (MVC)

CITATION: Indian MVC awarded as per The Gazette of India

"On 12 December 1947, Nand Singh was employed as a jemadar with the 1st Sikh Regiment, defending Kashmir from a Pakistani attack. Performing his duty with 'valour leadership and selfless devotion to duty,' Jemedar Nand Singh led in the capture of a key objective, near Uri. He was killed shortly after the objective was taken. To recognise this bravery, he was awarded posthumously the Maha Vir Chakra by independent India. This VC and MVC pair is unique."

There is a statue of Nand Singh at Fauji Chowk in Bathinda

SIKH REGIMENT

Branch
British Indian Army, Indian Army

Active
1846 – Present

Engagements
Abyssinia
Iraq
Malaya
North Africa
Italy
Greece
Burma

Regimental Motto
'Nische kar apni jeet karon' : With determination, I'll bring triumph
Nische kar apni aron"

Regimental war cry
Jo Bole So Nihal, Sat Sri Akal said :
"He who cries God is truth, is ever Happy."

Sikh troops in action. IWM/SE3267

Singh was posthumously awarded the Maha Vir Chakra (MVC), for valour and steadfastness of the highest order in the Jammu & Kashmir Operation in 1947. To this day no other Indian has received both the VC and MVC.

Project: For your eyes only

 Sikhism is a religion in India. Find out what other religions there are in India.

Did any of these religions have their own regiments in the Armed Forces such as the Sikh Regiment during WWII? The British and Commonwealth forces would have a chaplain, pastor or spiritual leader within their troops; what would their role be?

India 47

PEOPLE PROFILE Squadron Leader Karon Krishna Majumdar (DFC)

India's only IAF officer to receive 2 Distinguished Flying Cross medals

IWM/CL1176

FACT FILE
- **D.O.B.** 6 September 1913
- **D.O.D.** 17 February 1945
- **Years of service** 1934—1945
- **Rank** Wing Commander
- **Unit** No.1 Squadron, RIAF
- **Battles/Wars** Burma, France
- **Awards** 2 Distinguished Flying Cross (DFC) medals
- **Nickname** Jumbo

Squadron Leader Majumdar trained at RAF Cranwell and became a flying officer.

He flew a variety of aircraft including the Westland Wapiti and the Hawker Hart. Majumdar was quickly identified as having leadership skills and became a flight commander. He was promoted to squadron leader in June 1941. After the Japanese attacked Pearl Harbor and Malaya, Majumdar and his No.1 Squadron were posted to Burma.

They reached the Toungoo airfield on 1 February 1942 and the following day it was attacked by the Japanese Air Force. The assault destroyed and damaged Allied planes and only the No.1 Squadron's planes remained intact. In response, Majumdar immediately planned an attack on the Japanese at their airfield at Mae-Haungsan.

The next day, Majumdar took off on a solo mission in a Lysander armed with two 250lb 9113.4kg) bombs.

New Zealanders of the No. 67 RAF Squadron, who were also at the Toungoo airfield, sent an escort of two Buffalo fighters. Majumdar's surprise attack on the Japanese airfield was a success. He dropped his bombs with deadly accuracy, destroying a hangar and all the planes inside.

Inspired by his actions, the entire squadron returned to Mae-Haungsan the next day on a bombing mission. They successfuly destroyed several buildings, wireless installations and aircraft on the ground.

Majumdar's bravery earned him the Distinguished Flying Cross (DFC) during the Burma campaign. He was the first Indian officer to be decorated with the DFC during World War II.

Westland Wapiti Mark IIA aircraft flying in formation over the North West Frontier of India.
IWM/HU70781

Hawker Typhoon Mark IB undergoing servicing. Two dummy bombs used for practice loading onto the wing racks, can be seen in the foreground.
IWM/TR1091

Majumdar was awarded a second DFC in January 1945 (known as a 'Bar' to his DFC) during his posting to No 268. RAF Squadron.

On his return to India, Majumdar joined the Royal Indian Air Force air shows. He toured the country and took part in various aerobatic routines and displays.

On 17 February 1945, Majumdar went for a practice run in a Hawker Hurricane which was known for its mechanical problems. In the middle of a routine which involved a dive, one of the undercarriage legs unlocked itself, unbalancing the plane and causing it to stall. Majumdar crashed headlong into the ground and was killed instantly.

CITATION ONE
Distinguished Flying Cross - awarded as per *The London Gazette* dated 10 November 1942.

"*Early this year this officer commanded the squadron during its activities in Burma. He led two unescorted attacks on enemy airfields in Thailand and attacks in support of the army in Tennasserim; he also completed valuable reconnaissances during the retirement from Rangoon to the Prome positions.*"

CITATION TWO
Bar to Distinguished Flying Cross - awarded as per *The London Gazette* dated 23 January 1945.

"*This officer has completed many tactical reconnaissance and photographic sorties.*

His keenness for operational work and his skill on difficult and dangerous missions has always been outstanding. Before the advance northwards in France, he completed exceptionally valuable photographic reconnaissances of the Seine bridges, in the face of heavy ground defences.

He has also participated in long tactical reconnaissances on which he was several times intercepted by superior formations of enemy aircraft. His skill and courage have always been outstanding."

Project: For your eyes only

COVER STORY.
You are a group captain in the RAF.

Write a letter to your superiors nominating Squadron Leader Majumdar for a bravery award for his part in the events of 3 February 1942. Outline why he deserves to be honoured.

India 49

PEOPLE PROFILE
Assistant Section Officer Noor Inayat Khan GC

The first female radio operator to be sent into occupied France to aid the French Résistance

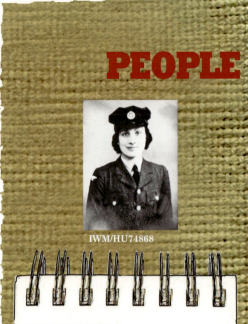

IWM/HU74868

FACT FILE
Code names
Jeanne Marie Renier
Nora Baker
Madeleine / W/T operator Nurse
Agent Phono (callsign: nurse)
D.O.B. 1 January 1914
Moscow, Russia
D.O.D. 13 September 1944
P.O.D. Dachau Concentration Camp
Service/branch
Women's Auxiliary Air Force (WAAF)
Special Operations Executive (SOE)
First Aid Nursing Yeomanry (FANY)
Years of service
1940—1944 (WAAF)
1943—1944 SOE
Rank Assistant Section Officer (WAAF)/Ensign (FANY)
Unit Physician
Awards
George Cross
MBE
Croix de Guerre (France)
Mentioned in Despatches
Other work
Poet and writer of children's stories including a book of traditional Indian stories 'Twenty Jakata Tales'

Noor Inayat Khan was born in Russia to an Indian father and American mother. Her paternal great-great-great grandgather was Tipu Sultan, the 18th century Muslim ruler who died in a struggle against the British.

Shortly before the outbreak of World War I her family moved to England, and later on settled in Paris, France. In May 1940 France was invaded by Germany. Just before the French surrendered, Khan escaped to England with her mother and sister.

In England Khan joined the Women's Auxiliary Air Force (WAAF) and trained as a wireless operator. Her ability to speak French fluently led to her recruitment by the Special Operations Executive (SOE) as a special agent (see page 33). Under the codename 'Madeleine' she was sent to Paris with other SOE agents in June 1943 and was constantly on the run from the Gestapo. Unfortunately, she was betrayed by an informer and arrested by the Gestapo who interrogated her for over a month.

While she did not reveal any information to her captors, they found her notebooks, inside they found, copies of all the messages she had sent. Her security breach gave the Germans enough information to send false messages to London in an attempt to confuse the British. This led to the capture of three more agents being captured.

P.O.W

Project: For your eyes only

COVER STORY. It's June 1943, you are a secret agent about to be sent to France to help the French Resistance.
Your cover story is that you are Jeanne Marie Renier, a secretary at the Université de Paris. Your parents are Gérard and Anne Jeanne Renier who still live in your hometown of Châteauroux. It is compulsory that all French citizens have an identity card called a *carte d'identité*.

Design a French identity card to support your cover story, and remember to include an address in Paris.

Khan's Security Breach

It appears that Khan misunderstood operational orders 'to be extremely careful with the filing of your messages.' In military operations the word 'filing' means 'sending' (in the same way that a journalist files a story.) Instead she thought that she was supposed to keep a filing system.

Khan made several escape attempts which led to her being classified as 'highly dangerous'. She was moved to Germany in November 1943, imprisoned at Pforzheim and kept in solitary confinement.

Khan and three other female SOE agents were eventually transported to the Dachau concentration camp in September 1944 where they executed. Her last word was '*Liberté*', meaning 'liberty' or 'freedom.'

Noor Inayat Khan was posthumously awarded a French Croix de Guerre with Gold Star. She was also one of three World War II First Aid Nursing Yeomanry (FANY) members to be awarded the George Cross.

Noor means 'Light of womanhood'
Inayat is a family name.
Khan is an honorific denoting aristocratic birth.

PRISONERS OF WAR (POWs)

FACT FILE

A **prisoner of war (POW) is a soldier or civilian who is taken prisoner by the enemy during or immediately after a war.**

The Allies, along with Germany and Italy, signed an international agreement called the Geneva Convention which stated they had to treat prisoners in a humane and respectful manner. The Convention covers all aspects of a prisoner's life including the food, which should be of a similar standard to that given to the captor's soldiers and not denied as a punishment. Prison camps should be hygienic, sanitary and provide medical facilities. Captors are also obliged to offer religious, sports and intellectual pursuits as well as to pay prisoners for any work undertaken.

Japan never signed this agreement. They often treated their prisoners brutally (see pages 53 and 55).

The prisoners' courtyard at Colditz Castle. IWM/HU20288

Many Indians were held captive by Axis forces in Europe, but Captain Birendra Nath Mazumdar, (pictured below) a Bengali doctor from the Royal Army Medical Corp, was the only Indian POW held at the notorious Colditz Castle, a high security German prison for captured Allied officers.

His German captors asked him many times to join the INA (see page 41) and even took him to meet Subhash Chandra Bose when he visited Berlin. Mazumdar refused to join, even though he wanted India to gain its independence from Great Britain.

He managed to escape from Colditz by staging a hunger strike which led to him being transferred to an all Indian prison camp. From there, along with two Indian soldiers, he escaped to London where he continued his work in the War by treating and caring for wounded Indian soldiers.

Captain Birendra Nath Mazumdar.

India 51

SECTION 2 INDIA and the FAR EAST

Unit 2: Ceylon

Albert Marshall, a fireman from Ceylon. He served with the Royal Navy in World War I, and with the Merchant Navy from the beginning of World War II. He also sailed on the Arctic route and to Africa and Malta.
IWM/D166 066

CEYLON, an island at the southern tip of India, is now known as Sri Lanka. It was a British colony and important to the Empire as a rubber producer.

At the start of the War, the Ceylon Defence Force and Ceylon Navy Volunteer Reserve were mobilised, while the Royal Navy and Royal Air Force used their existing installations on the island. Several Commonwealth units including Australian and African divisions were stationed in the city of Colombo throughout the War.

On 5 April 1942 the Japanese bombed the island causing the British naval fleet to retreat to East Africa.

Later, in 1942, a local anti-British political party encouraged some soldiers from the Ceylon Garrison Artillery in the Cocos Islands to rebel and join Bose's INA (see page 41). They were to hand over the islands to the Japanese. However the British authorities soon discovered the plot and executed three of the soldiers (mutineers) who had rebelled. They were the only British Commonwealth troops to be executed by the British during WWII. After this, no Ceylonese regiment was deployed by the British in a combat situation.

Ceylon's defences were strengthened with three Allied army divisions, and food rationing was brought in. This ensured that the local people were better fed than their Indian neighbours. The Allies hoped that this would keep the locals happy.

RAF ground crew and local Singhalese lowering a Consolidated Catalina of No. 240 Squadron RAF into the water at Red Hills Lake, Ceylon, after it underwent repairs.
IWM/CI876

Female labourers line up for bucket-loads of gravel, dug by the men, to repair the hard-standing areas of the flying boat station at Red Hills Lake, Ceylon. Parked behind them are Consolidated Catalina Mark IVs of No 240 Squadron RAF.
IWM/CI11006

Unit 3: BRITISH MALAYA and SINGAPORE

BRITISH MALAYA was made up of a series of states called the Straits Settlements, comprising Ponang, Malacca and Singapore the Federated Malay States and the Unfederated Malay States. It was colonised by the British between the 18th and 20th centuries. It was economically important as the world's largest producer of tin and rubber.

Japan invaded British Malaya in 1942 and occupied the area until 1945. British Malaya became independent in 1957, joining Singapore and North Borneo to form what is now called Malaysia in 1963. Singapore became independent in 1965

Flight Lieutenant C L F "Jimmy" Talalla of No.122 Squadron RAF, standing in front of his North American Mustang Mark III at B12/ Ellon, Normandy.

Born of Singhalese parents in Kuala Lumpur, British Malaya, Talalla joined the RAF in 1941 and served as a sergeant pilot with No.118 Squadron RAF, flying Supermarine Spitfires, before being commissioned in 1942.

He joined 122 Squadron as a flight commander in 1944 and finished the War having shot down five enemy aircraft.

His brother, Warrant Officer H C B Talalla, a Hawker Typhoon pilot serving with No. 182 Squadron RAF, was killed in action over the Falaise area on 25 July 1944.

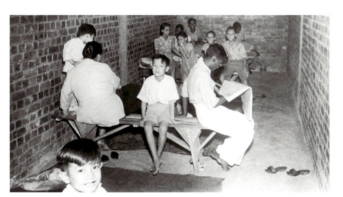

Civilians in a Singapore air raid shelter during a Japanese bombing raid. IWM/KF102

Children of Singapore cheer the arrival of the 5th Indian Division. IWM/SE4662

World War II British/Allied higher formation badge for Allied Land Forces, South East Asia. IWM/INS5021

The printing block used to produce the 'No Escape Pledge' form. IWM/EPH152A

The Selerang Barrack Square Incident, 30 August—5 September 1942, was brought about by the refusal of Allied POWs at Changi Gaol to sign a printed form declaring that they would not try to escape.

Allied soldiers agreed that they would not sign the form. As punishment 14,609 troops were confined in the barrack square at Selerang with reduced water rations.

Soon, the captives became distressed and poor hygiene led to some deaths. So the prisioners then agreed that they would sign the form, but only if it was made clear they were doing so under orders.
When signing, many of the Allied troops used false names – 'Ned Kelly' featured prominently for the Australians!

Ceylon and British Malaya and Singapore 53

SECTION 2 INDIA and the FAR EAST

Unit 4: Burma

BURMA, now known as Myanmar, is a country that sits between India and China. It is bordered to the north, west and east by high mountains. To the south lie the Bay of Bengal and Andaman Sea, and in the southeast Burma shares a border with Thailand, previously known as Siam.

From 1886 to 1948 Burma was under British control and part of British India. It was separated from India and became independent in 1937.

Some of the Burmese population resented the British as they believed the British did not like their culture. Despite their differences, some British settlers inter-mingled with the locals, creating an Anglo-Burmese population.

During World War II, Burma played a major part in the battles of South East Asia. To the British, Burma was a vital barrier protecting their 'jewel in the crown,' India, from the Japanese who had taken over China.

Burma was of huge strategic importance to the Japanese because its capture would allow them to invade and take over India. They could then join up with German forces who were invading the Middle East and finally shut down the Allies' supply line along the Burma Road into China.

A week after the attack on Pearl Harbor in the USA, the Japanese launched their invasion of British South East Asia. They successfully captured Singapore in February 1942 and, by March, Burma's capital, Rangoon, had fallen. Thirty thousand British troops withdrew along the Irrawaddy river and 600 miles of dense jungle and dangerous mountain passes.

When the British retreated from Burma they destroyed most of the port facilities so that the Japanese couldn't use them. However, the Sittang Bridge, the only escape route for an entire Indian division who were facing the Japanese, was also destroyed so the Indians were forced to swim across the river. Three thousand of them made it but many of the Gurkha brigade, (brave fighters from landlocked Nepal,) drowned as they had not learned to swim.

Men of the Madras Sappers stand before the gates of Fort Dufferin after the Japanese had fled. IWM/IND4549

So began the longest retreat in British military history, as Commonwealth forces fell back to India. It took nine weeks, with 4 000 lives lost and the remaining soldiers surviving on starvation rations. By the end of May, Burma was in

P.O.W

Soldiers of the Royal Garwhal Rifles search Japanese prisoners of war. IWM/IND4858

Japanese hands. Over the next year, the 14th Army was formed and, along with the Chindits prepared to recaptured Burma. These forces, in association with other Allies including a US-Chinese Army led by General Joseph Stilwell, went on the offensive.

Transport of the 5th Indian Division struggling through mud on the Tiddim Front. IWM/IND4058

The Allies relied on air support to drop in supplies and reinforcements to airlift casualties from jungle airstrips. Nearly 96% of the 14th Army's supplies were flown in during the Burma campaign.

The Allied attack on the Japanese, using jungle warfare and guerrilla tactics was successful. Finally, on 3 May 1945, Rangoon was back in British hands. Britain granted Burma its independence in 1948.

FACT FILE
1939 population 16,119,000
WWII military deaths 22,000
WWII civilian deaths 3,000

Between October 1942 and November 1943, Burmese civilians along with Allied POWs were forced by the Japanese to build the Burma-Thai railway. The railway was built through difficult jungle terrain in hostile conditions. Prisoners faced the possibility of contracting malaria, being bitten by poisonous snakes and brutal punishments from the Japanese.

If these prisoners did not work, the Japanese did not to feed them— despite the fact that this went against the Geneva Convention (see page 51.)

Over 100,000 people from many different countries lost their lives building the railway. These casualties are included in their country of origin statistics. It has been calculated that 400 men lost their lives for each mile of track laid. The line was about 260 miles long.

Project: For your eyes only

COVER STORY.
You are a lance corporal in the British Royal Marines and a POW in Burma.
You are forced by the Japanese to build the Burma-Thai Railway and you have seen many of your friends die.
Write a poem about your experiences.

Guerrilla tactics included blowing up railway lines, sabotaging Japanese military stores, destroying bridges and disrupting road transport.

Burma 55

PEOPLE PROFILES
Major Neville Hogan MBE

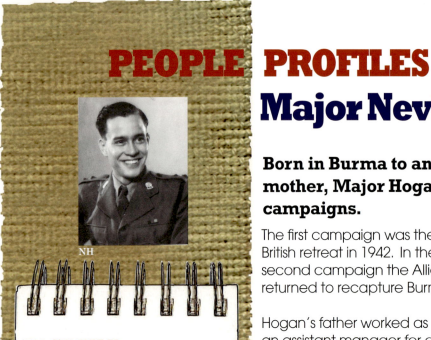
NH

Born in Burma to an Irish father and Burmese mother, Major Hogan fought in both Burma campaigns.

The first campaign was the British retreat in 1942. In the second campaign the Allies returned to recapture Burma.

Hogan's father worked as an assistant manager for a shipping company and his mother was a schoolteacher. He led an ordinary life with his two sisters (one of whom rose to the rank of major in the Women's Auxiliary Corps India (see page 43) in the British Indian Army) and a brother who eventually became an Anglican priest.

A keen boy scout, Hogan enlisted in the Territorial Army on 15 August 1939 at the tender age of 16. When war broke out in Europe, no one thought that the War would come to Burma and, like most young people, Hogan had no real interest in politics.

Everything changed when Singapore was captured by the Japanese and Burma became their next target. In early 1942 many civilians fled to India including Major Hogan's mother and siblings.

THE FIRST CAMPAIGN
The retreat from Burma to India was a gruelling operation. There was only one road to India. Much of the route was surrounded by hills or by paddy fields which were submerged in muddy water. The journey for Hogan and his troops covered about 1000 miles and took weeks to complete.

Once he arrived in central India, he was sent to Jhansi for infantry training in skills such as using a bayonet and other weapons. At this

Group photo taken at a jungle training camp, December 1944.
NH

time, Hogan also received a commission, which meant he was promoted from a private to an officer.

THE SECOND CAMPAIGN
Now an officer in the Burma Rifles, which formed the backbone of the Chindits, (see page 44) Hogan worked as a reconnaissance platoon

FACT FILE
D.O.B 24 July 1923
P.O.B Rangoon, Burma
Years of service
   1939—1950
Rank Major
Unit Burma Auxiliary
   Force (Territorial Army)
   Second Battalion
      Burma Rifles
   3rd (Chindit)
      Indian Infantry Division
Engagements
   1st Burma campaign
   2nd Burma campaign
Award
   MBE
Other work
   Clerk
   Salesman
   Chairman
      of the Chindits
      Old Comrades
      Association
   Hon. President of the
      Far Setting Sun
   Chairman of
      the Burma Welfare
      Association

commander. Along with other Allied troops, Hogan parachuted into Burma, deep inside enemy territory. Every day, Hogan and his unit had to go ahead of 400 men and 100 mules, looking for the best spots to receive supply drops from their air support crews.

They also had to find good landing sites where light planes could pick up casualties, locate food and water, and find places where 400 men and 100 mules could hide for the night. In addition, they had to clear the dung made by the mules and set booby traps for the enemy.

Major Hogan's fondest memories of this time were, "the camaraderie and friendship; knowing that you all shared the same experience, whether you were an officer or a private".

It was exhausting and painful, as the men were hunted like animals by the Japanese. They often had little sleep, little food and had to protect themselves from the tough terrain as well as their enemy. Mosquitoes carried the deadly disease malaria, and blood-sucking leeches would get inside their clothes.

In addition, each soldier had to carry their gun and a 55lb (24.9kg) backpack which contained food rations for five days, ammunition, a groundsheet, a cardigan, underwear, socks and a towel. On many occasions Major Hogan faced his biggest fear, which was hand-to-hand combat with the enemy. The Japanese attacked with rifles and Samurai swords. Hogan and his men would be forced to counterattack with their bayonets, while the Gurkhas used their *kukries*. Fighting was fierce and often fatal.

After the War Hogan remained in Burma, marrying his wife Glory in April 1949. However, the political tensions of a newly-independent Burma as well as anti-British sentiment, led to him being imprisoned by the Communist Party. He escaped and fled to England with his family in 1950 and is banned from returning to Burma. He lives with his family now in Hemel Hemstead, England.

Major Hogan was awarded an MBE on 1 January 2004 for his services to the Chindit Old Association and for providing welfare to war widows and disabled veterans.

Singer Dame Vera Lynn. IWM/P552

In 1944 famous singer, Dame Vera Lynn, met Major Hogan when he was just 21 years old and lying in a hospital bed in eastern India. Hogan was recovering from a bullet wound to his shoulder in addition to pneumonia, malaria and typhus.

Wedding day, 1949 NH

P.O.W

Major Hogan's wife Glory, who is also Anglo-Burmese, was a prisoner at a civilian POW Camp in Burma. Unlike most prisoners, Glory and her family were treated very well by their Japanese captors.

The Camp's commandment had been educated at Cambridge University in England and even apologised when he was ordered by his superiors not to give prisoners Red Cross relief parcels that were sent to them.

Major Hogan and his wife Glory in 2009. NH

She asked him if there was anything she could do for him and he asked for a kiss. She kindly obliged!

Dame Vera sang the wartime hits We'll Meet Again *and* There'll Be Bluebirds Over The White Cliffs of Dover *and was known as the 'Forces' Sweetheart'. She toured Egypt, India and Burma and performed outdoor concerts for the troops. In 2004, the pair met again at a 60th anniversary reception at London's Imperial War Museum.*

Burma 57

SECTION 3
Africa

FACT FILE*
1939 Population	42,000,000
Serving	372,000
Killed/missing in action	3,387
Wounded	5,549

*excludes Union of South Africa

Great Zimbabwe Ruins. GD

Traditional African mask.

Ancient Egyptian statue

Africa has a fascinating history. It is believed to be the birthplace of the entire human race. From 100,000 BC early humans from East Africa spread around the world evolving over time to make up the many different people we see today.

One of the world's oldest and greatest civilisations was based in Egypt in North Africa. The Egyptians left behind a glorious written history around 3,000 BC. They lived and worked with non-African civilisations such as the Phoenicians, who formed the merchant empire of Carthage, and the Romans who colonised North Africa in the 1st century BC.

By the 7th century AD Islam, practised by the Arabs, spread throughout North and East Africa as the Arabs traded with their neighbours in a variety of goods, including slaves. This led to the development of new cultures in East Africa such as those of the Swahili people and the Songhai Empire of Sub-Saharan West Africa. The Arabs also sailed down the east coast, founding states such as Mogadishu and Zanzibar.

From the 9th century the kingdom of Ghana ruled the West African region, it included those countries now called Mauritania and Mali. Mali became a separate Kingdom in the Middle Ages and was home to the fabled city of Timbuktu, where horses, gold, salt and slaves were sold. Other kingdoms, established at the same time, include Benin and Ife, Nigeria, which was known also for its terracotta sculptures and bronze heads.

In southern Africa about 1,430 impressive stone buildings were erected at Great Zimbabwe. In the late 15th century the

Portuguese began exploring Africa, and within a few years Europeans began to trade with Africans, leading to the notorious transatlantic slave trade. Europeans bought African slaves and took them to the Americas and the West Indies to work on plantations.

They also started to establish colonies in Africa. During the 16th and 17th centuries, the Portuguese settled in Angola and Mozambique, and the Dutch moved into South Africa.

While Europe banned the slave trade in the 1800s, at the same time they 'carved up' and colonised most of the continent. By the early 20th century, Africa was in European hands except for Liberia and Abyssinia, now known as Ethiopia.

During World War II more than 370,000 Africans fought alongside British, Indian and other Allied forces. Ninety thousand of them fought behind enemy lines in Burma as part of the Chindit and 14th Army operations

Africans from across the continent played their part including those from the Indian Ocean islands of Mauritius, Rodriguez and the Seychelles. With Africa's extensive coastlines, a naval presence was developed to protect territorial waters and Allied convoys. The Colonial Naval Volunteer Reserves was established to work alongside local naval forces.

Some Africans served with the Royal Air Force in the UK and Europe, while others served in local units. Thousands of civilians were employed to maintain air force bases.

After World War II the independence movement gathered momentum. Most African countries gained their freedom from colonial rule in the late 1950s and 1960s—except for Mozambique and Angola which became independent in 1975, and Zimbabwe, formerly known as Rhodesia, which gained independence in 1980.

Statue of Nelson Mandela in Parliament Square, London, England. DD

HOW AFRICA WAS CARVED UP PRE-WORLD WAR I

Great Britain's colonies
South Africa
Egypt
Rhodesia
(now Zimbabwe)
Northern Rhodesia
(now Zambia)
Nyasaland (now Malawi)
Uganda
Kenya
Ghana
Sierra Leone
Nigeria
Cameroon
British Somaliland

Portugal's colonies
Angola
Mozambique

Belgium's colonies
Belgian Congo
(now Democratic Republic of Congo)

France's colonies
Algeria
Madagascar
Morocco
Senegal
Côte d'Ivoire
Mali
Guinea
Burkina Faso
Benin
Niger

Germany's colonies
Burundi
Rwanda
Namibia
Togo
Cameroon
Tanzania

Italy's colonies
Libya
Italian Somaliland
Eritrea

Following World War II, South Africa introduced a racist policy called apartheid which forced people of different races to live separately and apart. Only white people were allowed to vote, live in certain areas and do certain jobs. South Africa's most famous anti-apartheid campaigner, Nelson Mandela, was imprisoned for 27 years. Around the world, most people came to condem apartheid.

By the late 1980s, many countries stopped trading with South Africa and its economy began to decline. The Government changed its policy and Mandela was later released from prison. He became South Africa's first black president in 1994.

Africa 59

SECTION 3

Unit 1: Union of South Africa

FACT FILE
1939 population 10,160,000
Military deaths 11,900
Civilian deaths due to war 0
Campaigns
North Africa
East Africa
Liberation of Malagasy, (now known as Madagascar)
Balkans
Romania
Poland
VC Medals 3

The traditional peoples of South Africa originate from the Khoikhoi, Bushmen and Bantu tribes from 5,000 years ago. Their descendants today are the Nguni people (the Zulu, Xhosa, Swazi and Ndebele) who settled near the coast, and the Sotho Tswana who settled in the Highveld. The Venda, Melba and Shangaan-Tsonga have all now established their domain in the north-eastern areas.

While the Portuguese were the first Europeans to discover South Africa, the Dutch were the first Europeans to colonise the territory in the 16th Century. Traders from the Dutch East Indies Company (in Dutch *Vereenigde Oostindische Compagnie,* or VOC) established the first permanent settlement in the south called the Cape. They imported slaves from Madagascar and Indonesia. Some of these slaves mixed with the Dutch settlers and their children became known as Cape Coloureds and Cape Malays.

As the VOC expanded their business and territory, they encroached on to the traditional lands of the Khoikhoi. The Dutch forcibly took their lands, introduced diseases to which the indigenous people had no immunity, and attacked them with their superior weapons. There were many wars between the Dutch and the indigenous people which lasted well into the 19th century. The Khoisan population

Zululand, South Africa, c. 1901—09. King Khambi (with arm outstretched), a subchief of the Dinizulu tribe, with his officers. The King and his men were fighting with British Empire forces against the Boers. AWMP0866002

was nearly wiped out. Surviving members were forced to work for the Dutch in unfair and unequal arrangements that bordered on slavery. Over time, some of the Khoisan people, Europeans and imported slaves intermingled creating people who were known as Coloureds.

The British arrived at the southern tip of South Africa in 1795 and established a colony called Cape Town. At the time there were 25,000 slaves, 20,000 white colonists, 15,000 Khoisans and 1,000 freed black slaves. Power was held by the whites and the idea of treating people differently according to the colour of their skin was accepted as normal. However there were also many differences between the whites, that is the Dutch Boers and the British. They spoke different languages (Afrikaans and English,) and the British dominated politics, trade, finance, mining and manufacturing, while the Boers were mostly farmers.

The Boers' anger over British control led to the Boer Wars. The first conflict started when diamonds and gold were discovered inland and the British quickly seized the territory. The first war lasted for three months and was followed by another which was much bloodier and lasted for three years. It ended in May 1902 with a British victory that cost 75,000 lives.

The British created a new country called the Union of South Africa. The Union was drawn into World War I and played a vital role in capturing two German colonies in West and East Africa, as well as providing refuelling stations and rest stops to the British Royal Navy. It also helped keep sea-lanes open to British India.

At the start of World War II, the South African Prime Minister, Barry Herzog, was leader of the pro-Afrikaner and anti-British National Party. He wanted to keep South Africa 'neutral' and not join the War. Opposing him was the former Prime Minister and soldier, Field Marshal Jan Smuts, who was pro-British and wanted to support the Allied effort.

The South African Parliament refused to accept Mr Herzog's point of view and removed him from office. He was replaced by Smuts on 4 September 1939.

Boer is the Dutch word for 'farmer.' It refers to those who speak Afrikaans and who, in the 18th century, left the Cape colony in the south, escaping British rule and settling in the northern states known as the Orange Free State and Transvaal. The Afrikaans language developed among the Dutch-speaking Protestant settlers from both the VOC colony and the slave workforce from Madagascar and Asia.

FAMOUS BOER WAR SOLDIERS INCLUDED
Winston Churchill who became the British Prime Minister during the War. (see page 86)
Sir Arthur Conan Doyle author of the Sherlock Holmes novels.
Lord Baden-Powell founder of the Boy Scouts.
Mahatma Gandhi leader of the India. independence movement.
Field Marshal Jan Smuts Prime Minister of South Africa.

Statue of Jan Smuts in Parliament Square, London, England DD

Right: Field Marshal Smuts standing in front of the aircraft in which he made his flying visits. It was an ex-South African Airways Lockheed Lodestar IWM TR5.

Far right: RAF cadets watching a Zulu war dance at Rose Deep Mine, Johannesburg in 1943 IWM TR1206

Once in power, Prime Minister Smuts immediately declared war against Germany. At this time there were only 3,353 men in the South African Army with a further 14,631 in the Active Citizen Force (ACF). However they were only trained and equipped solely for bush warfare within southern Africa.

South Africa had a serious shortage of available men to serve in the armed forces. There were two reasons for this. One was that the Government would only consider men of European descent aged between 20 and 40 years of age as eligible to serve; the other was that many Afrikaans people were anti-British and actively opposed to the War.

In order to free up the number of whites to fight and provide technical services, a number of units were created which allowed drivers and foot soldiers from the Cape Coloured and Asian populations to join up.

Units made up of blacks were also formed to provide labour. These units were not allowed to take part in fighting against Europeans.

Those people of non-European, coloured or black African heritage were only able to join the following special units:
Cape Corps for coloureds
Indian & Malay Corps for Asians
Native Military Corps for blacks

The South African authorities had a general policy of not providing these units with firearms, as they feared that the units could lead an armed uprising against them. Instead, the units were armed with traditional weapons such as *assegais* (spears) and *knobkierries* (clubs).

About 92,000 men volunteered and served in these units. A further 15,000—20,000 black Africans worked as casual labourers on various military bases throughout the country.

An NMC guards an aircraft at an air school in Pretoria, armed only with his assegai. *IWM TR1262*

> **!** The **Ossewabrandwag** (OB), which means Oxwagon Sentinel, was a nationalist Afrikaner political group founded in February 1939. The OB opposed South Africa's entry into World War II on the British side and wanted independence from Great Britain. They supported the Axis powers and modelled their paramilitary group called the *Stormjaers* or storm chasers on the Nazi SA (Storm troopers).
>
> Many members were imprisoned during the War for committing acts of sabotage and after the War some members became politicians, including John Vorster and P W Botha who went onto become South African Prime Ministers. The OB is believed to have been disbanded some time in the 1960s.

SPECIAL UNITS

Cape Corps

Name Cape Corps
Branch Union Defence Force
Active 1781—1990

The Cape Corps was the main military organisation in which the 'coloured' members of South Africa's population served. Between 1948 and 1963 it was disbanded as the government at the time abolished military service for Coloureds.

During World War II, the Cape Corps was non-combatant, meaning that its members did not fight against the enemy. They had a pioneer battalion which would perform duties such as laying roads, digging trenches and making bridges ahead of their army.

They also had several motorised infantry battalions, regular infantry battalions, prisoner-of-war guards and escort battalions. At its peak there were about 23,000 members of the Cape Corps. During the War the Indian and Malay Corps became a part of the Cape Corps.

Crown Princess Frederica of Greece inspecting the Guard of Honour of the Cape Corps on a visit to the South African Base Depot, Middle East Headquarters in January 1945
IWM MEM1991

Native Military Corps

Name Native Military Corps
Branch Union Defence Force
Active 1940—1945
Commander Lieutenant Colonel BW Martin

Originally called the Native Labour Corps which was formed on 1 June 1940, it later became known as the Native Military Guards Brigade and finally the Native Military Corps (NMC At its height, the NMC comprised 80,000 African recruits, with 10 battalions performing guard duties equipped with assegais.

Initially there were four battalions under the name of the Native Military Guards Brigade. These were drawn from Africans from across the country. The 1st battalion were from Zululand, the 2nd from northern Transvaal, the 3rd from Transkei and the 4th battalion, called the Witwatersrand Battalion, consisted of Africans from urban areas.

As they were not allowed to take combative or fighting roles, NMC members were trained in various support functions such as labouring, road building and as first-aiders. After their training they were posted to the battlegrounds of East Africa, Abyssinia, Egypt, Libya and Italy.

> Since 1994 coloured and black soldiers, sailors and airmen have served alongside their fellow South Africans in a fully integrated South African National Defence Force.

South Africa 63

PEOPLE PROFILES Lance Corporal Job Maseko MM

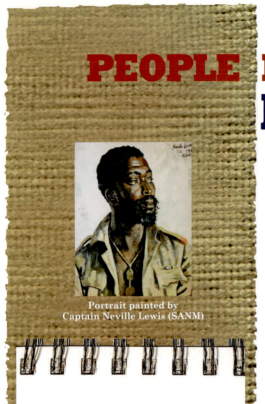

Portrait painted by Captain Neville Lewis (SANM)

FACT FILE
D.O.B	Unknown
P.O.B	Springs, South Africa
D.O.D	1952
Tribe	Zulu
Years of service	Unknown
Rank	Lance Corporal
Unit	Native Military Corps (NMC)
Branch	South African 2nd Infantry Division
Engagements	World War II North Africa
Awards	Military Medal (MM)
Other work	Delivery man Labourer

Prior to his enlistment, Lance Corporal Maseko worked as a delivery man in the town of Springs in what is now Gauteng, South Africa.

Maseko's father was angered by his decision to join the war effort. He asked him why he wanted to die for the white man. Maseko knew that some blacks felt that it was a 'white man's war.' But he chose to fight for his country and freedom, like thousands of other black South Africans.

Maseko initially volunteered for service with the NMC where he completed his basic training. As blacks and coloureds were not trained in the use of firearms, he was not given a gun. He was then transferred to North Africa with the South African 2nd Infantry Division.

In June 1942, at Tobruk, along with thousands of other Allied soldiers, he became a prisoner of war. In total 32,000 men were captured by the Germans, including 10,722 South Africans, of which 1,200 were fellow NMC members.

One night Maseko asked the Italian guards for washing water. They made a racist remark, suggesting that as he was already black, washing would make no difference. Maseko reacted angrily so they held him down and beat him.

While nursing his wounds, Maseko sat outside and punched the ground. Through the desert sands he felt something hard – it was a cartridge.* The prison camp had been built on battle debris and there was still a lot of rubbish lying around.

Prisoners, captured by the Germans during the siege of Tobruk, are escorted away with their hands on their heads. IWM MH5577

He kept searching and found 40 cartridges, pieces of fuse wire and a discarded milk tin. While cartridges without a gun were useless to him, the cordite, a type of gunpowder, inside the cartridge, could be used to blow something up. He could make a bomb.

With the help of his fellow soldiers, who created a diversion, Maseko was able to

*A cartridge is a casing containing an explosive charge and bullet.

plant his bomb on an enemy cargo ship, which they had been ordered to unload. The plan worked, the bomb went off and the ship sank. The Germans had no idea how it happened or who was responsible.

A week or so later, Maseko and his friend Private Masiya escaped from Tobruk. They walked across the desert for 23 days and were found by South African and British troops on 16 November 1942, just south of El Alamein.

After the War, when Maseko returned home, he was denied his promised military pension. In terms of race relations, nothing had changed in South Africa. He then worked as a labourer on the railways and he died penniless in 1952.
He was buried in the Payneville Township Cemetery of Springs.
His funeral was paid for with borrowed money.

According to Captain Neville Lewis, the first official war artist for South Africa during the World War II, Job Maseko was recommended for a Victoria Cross but, being 'only an African', he was awarded the Military Medal instead.

In 2007, South African director Vincent Moloi made a documentary film about Job Maseko and the South Africa 2nd Infantry Division called "A Pair of Boots and a Bicycle".

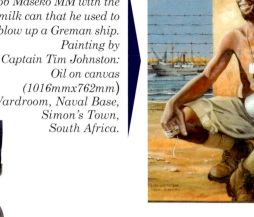

Lance Corporal Job Maseko MM with the milk can that he used to blow up a Greman ship. Painting by Captain Tim Johnston: Oil on canvas (1016mmx762mm) Wardroom, Naval Base, Simon's Town, South Africa.

CITATION

"For meritorious and courageous action in that on or about the 21st July, while a Prisoner of War, he, Job Masego (sic), sank a fully laden enemy steamer - probably an "F" boat - while moored in Tobruk Harbour.

This he did by placing a small tin filled with gunpowder in among drums of petrol in the hold, leading a fuse therefrom to the hatch and lighting the fuse upon closing the hatch.
In carrying out this deliberately planned action, Job Masego displayed ingenuity, determination and complete disregard of personal safety from punishment by the enemy or from the ensuing explosion which set the vessel alight."

The South African Navy named two units, a ship and the Simon's Town Naval Base Wardroom after him. The community of Kwa Thema near Springs named a primary school after him as well as the main road linking the town of Springs to KwaThema Township.

Project: For your eyes only

Write a poem, song or rap about Maseko getting the better of the Germans from blowing up the ship and escaping from the POW camp.

Also include the difficulties he faced as a black South African and not being allowed to carry a firearm.

South Africa 65

PEOPLE PROFILES Lance Corporal Lucas Majozi DCM

FACT FILE
D.O.B 1916
P.O.B Zastron, Orange Free State, South Africa
D.O.D 1969
Tribe Zulu
Years of service Unknown
Rank Lance Corporal
Unit Native Military Corps (NMC)
Branch 1/2 Field Force
Engagements World War II North Africa
Awards Distinguished Conduct Medal (DCM)
Other work Police Sergeant

Lucas Majozi served with the Native Military Corps during WWII at the Battle of El Alamein, North Africa.

As a black African in the South African army, he was not allowed to engage in direct combat with the enemy or carry a gun. He served instead as a stretcher-bearer, meaning that he was a first-aid attendant who picked up wounded soldiers and took them away from the battlefield to receive medical attention.

During the long battle of El Alamein in North Africa, which started on 23 October 1942, the Allies had to attack enemy forces. The South Africans needed to get through a minefield which the Germans had sown with more than 500,000 mines.

As the 1/2 Field Force Battalion forced its way through, they were attacked by heavy machine-gun and artillery fire from German troops led by their commandant Field Marshal Erwin Rommel.

The battalion suffered severe casualties, many of whom needed urgent medical care and had to be removed from the combat zone. Majozi bravely tended his white, wounded comrades and carried them off the battlefield. He worked hard all through the night despite being shot at by the Germans. At one point Majozi was injured, but he continued to do his job. If it weren't for the bravery of Majozi and his team of stretcher-bearers, many more men would have died from their injuries.

Major-General Daniel Hermanus Pienaar, the commander of the 1st South African Division, said of Majozi:

"This soldier did most magnificent and brave things. With a number of bullets in his body he returned time after time into a veritable hell of machine gun fire to pull out wounded men. He is a man of whom South Africa can well be proud. He is a credit to his country."

For his bravery Majozi was awarded the Distinguished Conduct Medal, the highest honour given to a black South African soldier during World War II.

After the War, Majozi returned to Zastron and joined the South African Police. He died in 1969. His medal can be seen at the South African National Museum of Military History, along with his portrait painted by South African war artist Captain Neville Lewis.

CITATION

"On the night of October 23-24, Majozi accompanied his company into action as a stretcher-bearer. In the later stages of the action when he was within 100 yards of the enemy and under heavy fire, he thought nothing of his personal safety and continued to evacuate casualties assisted by co-bearers. He was then wounded by shrapnel, but he continued evacuating the wounded. Told by a medical corporal to go back to the regimental aid post, he replied that there were many wounded men still in the minefield.

He went back, and with the assistance of other stretcher-bearers, he brought back more wounded. After his co-bearer had become a casualty, he did not waver, but carried wounded men back alone on his back to the aid post.

When he was eventually told by the Company Commander to go back, he smilingly refused and remained on duty, working incessantly till he collapsed next morning through sheer exhaustion, stiffness, and loss of blood. His extreme devotion to duty and gallant conduct under continuous enemy fire throughout the night saved the lives of many wounded men who would otherwise have died through loss of blood or possible further wounds."

Portrait of Lucas Majozi in his uniform as a stretcher bearer painted by Captain Neville Lewis SANM.

Majozi has a street named after him in Zastron, South Africa

Soldiers of the South African Native Military Corps issued with assegais instead of rifles.

Project: For your eyes only

You are a medical orderly. You must tend to the wounded casualties that Majozi and his team are bringing in. Make a sling, an eye patch and a leg splint for your injured colleagues and practise your first-aid.

South Africa 67

SECTION 3
Unit 2: British Southern Africa

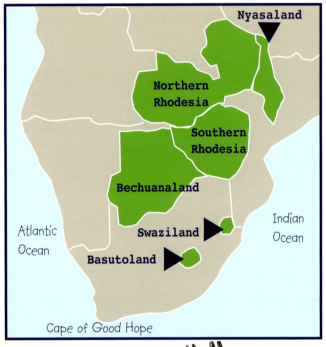

FACT FILE
Here British Southern Africa refers to
Northern Rhodesia (now Zambia)

Southern Rhodesia (now Zimbabwe)

Nyasaland (now Malawi)

Bechuanaland (now Botswana)

Basutoland (now Lesotho)

Swaziland

At the outbreak of war, British Southern Africa eagerly answered Britain's call to arms In fact some tribal chiefs even offered troops against potential white rebellion in South Africa after declaring their allegiance to the King. This was because South Africa initially wished to remain neutral. Smuts then replaced Hertzog as prime minister and South Africa entered the War.

By 1941 the British army were desperately short of men and in the Middle East they were stretched to the limit. The British planned to mobilise indigenous Africans in British Southern Africa by creating a new military unit which would be completely separate from South Africa's Native Military Corp. This was highly controversial, as they faced pressure from South Africa to prohibit blacks from holding firearms.

On the African homefront a group of women from Palapye, Bechuanaland, knit clothes for the Navy League. IWM SAF205

Talks were held between British, South Africans and native chiefs, and agreement was reached to establish the African Auxiliary Pioneer Corp (AAPC).

Features of the AAPC:
- British officers were in command and control of AAPC personnel
- All personnel had to swear an oath of allegiance to the Crown
- Military service could be anywhere in the world
- AAPC was separate from South Africa's NMC
- More than a quarter of AAPC men were armed for self-defence

WHY DID THEY FIGHT?
Over 35,000 Africans joined the AAPC for many reasons including:
- **loyalty** to the British crown
- **duty** to follow their tribal chiefs
- **regular pay**
- to gain an **education** or improve their **literacy skills**
- to seek **new experiences** and **adventure**

Members of the AAPC built roads, were camp guards and built fortifications against Axis invasion. They also served as heavy artillery gunners, specialist bridge-builders, camouflage smoke-makers, drivers, mechanics and front-line supply store shifters.

The unit was known as the African Auxiliary Pioneer Corps until 5 October 1944. It became known as the African Pioneer Corps until 1947, before being disbanded in 1949.

The men of the Basotho companies were great singers and they composed songs about their war experiences. Here is a song about the ship *Erinpura* and their voyage to Malta. Sadly, on 1 May 1943, the troopship *Erinpura* was sunk by a German air attack in the Mediterranean with the loss of 943 lives; of these 633 were Basotho soldiers of the African Auxiliary Pioneer Corps.

ERINPURA VOYAGE TO MALTA

The day we were bound for Malta
Ships were sunk
By the German flying birds
They thundered! thunder! thunder!
Bombard
Bombard! Bombard! thundered!

Commander Monty was notified
Matters have worsened at sea.
The Junkers planes of the enemy
Have escaped unseen by guard at Tunisia
They fired with torpedoes
Although the matters are thus
We are determined to reach there

Telegraphs were dispatched
Throughout the world
The people mourned for the north
They were gripped by sorrowful fear
Services sounded in all the troops
'You shall hear Hitler
When No 4 is fired'.

All commanders of war assembled in Cairo
To confer about new manoeuvre
The Italians stamped about
Stating that they had seen flares of cannons - artilleries
That was No 4, coughing in the wilderness

Masoulin lowered his flags on all sides unconditionally
Struck by the army brigade
Died, the death of a gun his verdict
This was court martials
The severe court of war.

Look out you Rommel
They are now facing you
Those of Monty and the allied
Hear them roaring, bombarding all over
The earth shaking dust blustered up
Those were the artillery
Fired by Ntsebo's sisters
With those of the English.

At Matsieng, Mokethoaneng
Fortress place of Seeiso
Mantsebo the Chief of Basotho
Was crowned a warrior
Her name appeared in dispatch
Among the allied people
Displayed in all their courts.

SPECIAL UNITS

Rhodesian African Rifles

Name	Rhodesian African Rifles (RAR)
Branch	Rhodesian Army
Mascot	'Private N'duna' the goat
Active	1916—1981
Engagements	World War I
	World War II
	Suez Crisis
	Malayan Emergency
	Nyasaland
	Northern Rhodesia
	Congo Border
	Rhodesian Bush War

Previously formed as the Rhodesian Native Regiment during World War I, the RAR served in World War II during the 1940s, and during 1966 – 1973 in the Rhodesian Bush War, with black non-commissioned officers and white officers. During World War II, the RAR was based at Salisbury in Rhodesia. The RAR fought with the Allies in Burma in 1944 and served alongside the King's African Rifles from East Africa.

After Rhodesia gained independence the RAR were integrated into the Zimbabwe National Army.

A painting by Leslie Cole of soldiers from Bechuanaland cleaning anti-aircraft guns in the twilight after action, Syracuse, Sicily. IWM ART_LD4576

African Auxiliary Pioneer Corps

Name	African Auxiliary Pioneer Corps, African Pioneer Corps
Branch	British Army
Active	1941—1949
Engagements	British East Africa
	North Africa
	Malta
	Italy
Awards	Member of British Empire (MBE)
	Military Medal (MM)
	British Empire Medal (BEM)
	Mentioned in Despatches
	Commendations

RAF mechanics attend to the engine of a De Haviland Tiger Moth at Salisbury, Southern Rhodesia. while local personnel clean the aircraft. IWM CM1183

A Sherman tank drives over a newly-laid road surface, constructed over soft ground by African Auxiliary Pioneer Corps in Italy. IWM NA8930

Swaziland

Swazi Pioneers

Name: Swazi Pioneers
Active: 1941—1945
Branch: African Auxiliary Pioneer Corps
Engagements: Palestine
Syria
North Africa
Sicily
Italy
Commander: Colonel Herbert Johnson OBE MC TD

Swaziland is one of the smallest countries in Africa yet still its people answered Great Britain's call to join the War.

Colonel Johnson was appointed to recruit 1,000 Swazi men to the African Auxiliary Pioneer Corps. He believed the Swazi people had many admirable qualities and was deeply respectful of their culture. So King Sobhuza II of Swaziland gave his permission and immediately Johnson succeeded in recruiting more than 1,000 men, Johnson took a keen interest in his men's welfare. The Swazis were trained as motor mechanics, carpenters, tailors and hospital orderlies and those that were illiterate were taught to read and write. Johnson wanted to ensure that they had skills which would help them after the War. Once the men had finished their training, they were sent on active service. Johnson promised King Sobhuza that the Swazis would never be split up. He kept that promise and the Swazis remained together throughout the War.

The Swazis served in Palestine, Syria, North Africa, Sicily and Italy mainly in port operations handling hazardous consignments of ammunition and fuel, often under enemy fire. They also provided smokescreens during air raids. The Swazis were the only indigenous Africans to serve in the Italian Campaign of Anzio and in June 1944 they were among the first to enter Rome after the assault troops. The first Swazi soldier to receive an award was Sergeant-Major Mfunda Sukati, who was mentioned in despatches.

After the German surrender in 1945, Colonel Johnson was posted away from his Swazi Pioneers. Before he left he told them: *"I salute you and thank you for your loyal service. Only those who have been with you all the time know the extent of your value to the war effort. The name 'Swazi' is known and respected far and wide, thanks to you... All my days I will remember you with pride and affection."*

In reply the troops wrote: *"The Swazis have heard with regret the news of your departure and read with sorrow your farewell to us...we have looked forward to the end of the war, when we would be able to return to our homes... For the fact that we can do so with pride in our achievements, we salute you. For the happiness that has been ours, due to your just but kindly treatment, we thank you... You were not merely our colonel, you were our father. You were not merely our commanding officer, you were our friend... we can be thankful only to you, sir, that many of us can return home competent in various trades... We shall remember you with love and loyalty in the future... We shall be proud and pleased, if the future again sees Colonel Johnson meeting the Swazis under the trees at Lobamba Royal Kraal."*

Sadly Colonel Johnson was unable to visit Swaziland again but he and his wife did form the Colonel Johnson Educational Trust for Swaziland. In 1984. When he died in 1984 he left almost £7,000 to the trust. His wife gave the trust £52,000 (most of her savings} before she died in 1991 and left the remainder to it in her will.

Soldiers move through a smokescreen. IWM NA 010937

British Southern Africa

SECTION 3
Unit 3: West Africa

FACT FILE
Countries in British West Africa:
Nigeria
Gold Coast
 (now Ghana)
British Togoland
 (now Ghana)
Gambia
Sierra Leone
British Cameroon

Engagements
Italian Somaliland
Abyssinia
Burma

Throughout the 18th century, Britain and France established trading posts along the west african coast. By the early 1900s, all of them had become their colonies, with the exception of Liberia which was never colonised.

In 1940 France was taken over by the Germans and Italians. The Free French government in exile, led by General Charles de Gaulle, fought against them. But there were other French people who joined the Germans and fought with them. They formed the Vichy government led by Marshal Philippe Pétain. This posed a problem for French African colonies who had to choose which side to support, and also for the British who feared invasion of their West African colonies by Vichy forces. Many French Equatorial territories' governors declared their loyalty to the Free French forces and Congo-Brazzaville became a temporary capital for Free France.

French North Africa and French West Africa chose to support the Vichy regime. However, when the Allies regained control of North Africa, French West African colonies switched sides and supported the Free French government.

Aside from protecting Great Britain's African colonies, the British needed more soldiers to fight in the Middle East and Asia. Initially they recruited policemen and government workers such as drivers. Many Africans volunteered but some were forced to join the army by their chiefs who worked with the British.

Some 90,000 troops from West and East Africa fought in Burma against the Japanese as part of the Chindits. They were dropped into jungle airstrips in the Kaladan peninsula by glider to attack the Japanese deep behind enemy lines. The Kaladan peninsula was covered in jungle and criss-crossed by high mountain ridges and fast rivers called *chaungs*. There were no roads, so the soldiers received all their supplies by air.

Great Britain's No.91 Squadron RAF flew Supermarine Spitfires which had been bought with money from the people of Nigeria. All the Spitfires were named after Nigerian provinces and the squadron became known as the No.91 (Nigeria) Squadron. Here Squadron Leader Oxspring stands on the wing of his plane called 'Nigeria Oyo Province.'
IWM CH5444

After supplies were dropped, the troops had to find and secure them before the Japanese did. They then had to carry them on their heads, marching up to 30 miles a day with huge loads of food, ammunition and equipment. The Africans learnt the art of jungle warfare from their Japanese enemies. They carried their own supplies so they were highly mobile in the jungle. They were able to mentally and physically deal with both the difficult terrain and intense hand-to-hand combat, and were less susceptible to the heat and tropical diseases than their British counterparts.

Many Africans believed in *'ju-ju'*, which means magic. They carried lucky charms and wore special necklaces that they believed protected them from enemy bullets. Some even believed these items made them invisible. The British spread rumours that African soldiers were not only strong and impressive, but also ate people. This was to make the Japanese soldiers afraid.

The African troops spent much time in India serving alongside Indian soldiers and were duely influenced by India's independence campaign. This made them think long and hard about their own country leading to far-reaching change.

The Gold Coast and British Togoland became the independent country of Ghana In 1957. Nigeria gained independence in 1960. The northern part of the British Cameroons became part of Nigeria while the southern part, which had been a French colony, became the independent country of Cameroon in 1961. Sierra Leone also gained independence in 1961 and the Gambia became independent a few years later, in 1965.

THE WEST AFRICAN CAMPAGN

The West African campaign refers to two battles fought in the region. The Battle of Dakar and the Battle of Gabon both occurred in late 1940 and involved Allied forces attacking Vichy forces. Once Gabon was captured by Free French troops, the French maintained control of AEF (see box below). However AOF (below) remained under Vichy control until 1942.

OTHER COUNTRIES IN THE REGION

Liberia

French West Africa
Afrique Occidentale Française (AOF)
- **Senegal**
- **Togo**
- **Guinea**
- **Benin**
- **Mauritania**
- **Mali**
- **Burkina Faso**
- **Côte D'Ivoire**

French Equatorial Africa
Afrique-Equatoriale Française (AEF)
- **Chad**
- **Central African Republic**
- **Congo-Brazzaville**
- **Gabon**
- **Niger**
- **Cameroun**

In Ghana and Sierra Leone, the defeat of the Japanese forces at Myohaung in Burma is celebrated every year on 24 January—Myohaung Day.

West Africa 73

LIBERIA

Liberia was officially neutral until 27 January 1944 when the country declared war on Germany. However, until that time, it did allow the Allies access to its territory as a transit point for troops and resources enroute to North Africa. Before the USA joined the war their ships were registered under the Liberian flag. This allowed them to appear to be neutral, while supplying the Allies. After they entered the War, the Robertsfield Airport was built to enable B47 bombers to refuel, making it the longest runway in Africa to this day.

Liberia also provided the Allies with a major source of rubber during the War as the plantations in South East Asia were taken over by the Japanese.

ENLIST TODAY!
Your country needs you!
Not for learning how to shoot the big howitzers
Or how to rat tat tat the machine guns
Or how to fly o'er peaceful countries
Dropping bombs on harmless people
Or how to fix a bayonet and charge at
The harmless workers of another clime

Your country needs you
For the rebuilding of your shattered homeland —
Your homeland ruined by exploitation
By the tyrants of foreign nations
Who would use you as their catspaw
While they starved you to subjection
— *African Standard, 28 July 1939.*

! OPPOSING VIEW !
Wallace Johnson, a political activist and editor of the *African Standard* newspaper in Sierra Leone openly criticised the British and believed that the War only served the interest of capitalism and colonialism. The British imprisoned him in 1939 and released him in 1944.

SPECIAL UNITS

Royal West African Frontier Force

Name	Royal West African Frontier Force (RWAFF)
Active	1900—1960
Engagements	East Africa Burma
Commander	General Sir George James Giffard

The RWAFF was initially formed to garrison the British West African colonies. Included in the force were the Nigeria Regiment, Gold Coast Regiment, Sierra Leone Battalion and Gambia Company.

Standard weapons included the .303 Martini Enfield carbine with QF 2.95 inch mountain guns (quick-firing howitzers) for the artillery.

RWAFF parade uniform included a khaki drill, red caps called fezes (shown above) and scarlet zouave-style jackets with red cummerbunds. The badge on the fez was a palm tree.

In 1957 when the Gold Coast gained independence, the Gold Coast Regiment withdrew to form the Ghana Regiment of Infantry. As the other countries were seeking their own independence, the RWAFF disbanded in 1960.

Royal West African Frontier Force in Kenya. IWM E2003

81st (West Africa) Division

Name: 81st (West Africa)
Active: 1943—1945
Branch: Royal West African Frontier Force
Engagements: Burma
Commander: Major General Frederick Joseph Loftus-Tottenham

The Division was created by General Giffard during World War II from units of the West African Frontier Force. One of the brigades joined the Chindits while the remainder joined the XV Indian Corps, 14th Army and 82nd (West Africa) Division all taking part in the 2nd Burma Campaign.

The formation badge had a black spider design. This represented 'Gizzo' or 'Anansi', a character from Ashanti mythology who overcame his enemies by using clever tactics. The badge was worn head down so it would appear to be going forward when a soldier was about to fire his weapon.

"Their discipline and smartness were impressive, and they were more obviously at home in the jungle than any troops I had yet seen." Field Marshal Sir William Slim

Indian soldiers mingle with men of the 81st West African Division after the latter had arrived in India for jungle training. The first African colonial troops to fight outside Africa, the 81st Division went on to Burma in December 1943.IIND2864

82nd (West Africa) Division

Name 82nd (West Africa) Division
Active 1941—1945
Branch Royal West African Frontier Force
Engagements Burma Campaign
Commanders Major General George McIlree Stanton Bruce, Major General Hugh Charles Stockwell

This Division was also formed by General Giffard. It was sent to Burma in July 1944. The formation badge shows two spears crossed on a native carrier's headband which symbolised 'through our carriers we fight'. This showed the important role the carriers played in moving supplies for the division; they even carried 3.7in howitzers. During the third Arakan campaign in Burma, the 82nd Division suffered the highest casualties of any unit in the XV Corps – more than 2,000 African soldiers died. This was because they fought at such close quarters in the jungle with the enemy that it was very difficult to provide artillery and air support.

Some of those killed were simply buried in the jungle, many others were buried in cemeteries at the Dalet Chaung near Tamandu and the Taukkyan War Cemetery. Others are remembered at the War Memorial in Rangoon.

A 3.7-inch howitzer in action against the Japanese in Burma. IWM SE358

West Africa 75

PEOPLE PROFILES Major Seth Kwabla Anthony MSG, MBE

First black African commissioned into the British Army

NAM

FACT FILE
- **D.O.B** 15 June 1915
- **P.O.B** Accra, Ghana
- **D.O.D** 20 November 2008
- **Years of service** 1939—1945
- **Rank** Major
- **Unit** 81st Division Royal West African Frontier Force (RWAFF)
- **Branch** British Army
- **Engagements**
  - World War II
  - 2nd Burma Campaign
- **Awards** Member of the Order of the Star of Ghana (MSG)
  - Burma Star
  - MBE
  - Mentioned in several despatches
- **Other work**
  - Teacher
  - Diplomat

Born in Accra and educated at the Bremen Mission School in Keta, Major Anthony trained as a teacher in Latin, English and mathematics.

In early 1939 he became a part-time soldier with the Gold Coast Territorial Force of the RWAFF. As an educated African he was able to apply for a position as an officer cadet, which he duly did and within three months rose to the rank of Cadet Sergeant.

By September 1939, Anthony was ready for war. His battalion was involved in guarding Takoradi harbour and operating coastal defences, as this was where British aircraft destined for the North African campaign were shipped and assembled.

Anthony was an excellent soldier and leader. He was the first black African to be sent for officer training at the Royal Military College, at Sandhurst, England, in November 1941.

While he was the only black man in the College he quickly adapted to his new environment as he was determined to win his commission, which he did on 2 April 1942. He gained the rank of second lieutenant and returned home to Ghana.

Officer cadets march in a Passing Out parade at the Royal Military College, Sandhurst. IWM TR7216

Anthony was also involved in training many of the 65,000 Ghanaians who fought for Britain. Nearly half of these fought abroad, helping to liberate Somaliland and Abyssinia, as well as defeating the Japanese at Myohaung in Burma.

On his arrival back in Accra, he was called up for service in Burma. On the way there, his troopship carrying the troops berthed in South Africa. While on shore leave he went to join some of his white friends in a pub, but the white landlady refused to serve him. The other officers

Major Anthony receives his Burma Star from Viscount Slim.

RWAFF veterans in Ghana, 2008.

told her that he was an officer of the King's army and should therefore be treated with respect, but she still refused to serve him because he was black. His friends got very angry but Anthony quietly left, not wishing to cause any trouble.

Many RWAFF soldiers believed in *ju-ju* and those in Burma believed that Anthony had been blessed by a *ju-ju* man or witchdoctor. As a result they believed that he and his men would be protected from enemy bullets.

They also believed that he had the power to make himself invisible to the Japanese because Anthony was skilled at getting behind enemy lines without being seen. He would attack them and then instantly disappear back into the jungle. Similarly to the Australian Special Units (see page 16), Anthony and his men also knew how to live off the land and support themselves.

The Africans were to prove very strong fighters against the Japanese in jungle warfare, and prooved themselves valuable to the Allied campaign in Burma.

After the War, Anthony rode triumphantly in an open car with Field Marshal Lord Montgomery through the streets of London at a victory parade. He was then given a position in the civil service in Ghana as the Assistant Secretary at the Ministry of the Interior.

Once Ghana gained independence, Anthony became a diplomat and opened the first Ghanaian embassy in the USA. He also served at the United Nations.

Anthony retired from public service in 1973. In 2007 he was awarded one of Ghana's highest honours, the Member of the Order of the Star of Ghana (MSG). In July 2008 Viscount Slim, President of the Burma Star Association and the son of Field Marshal Sir William Slim of the 14th Army travelled to Ghana and presented Anthony with the Burma Star Badge.

Major Seth Kwabla Anthony died in Accra in November 2008 and left behind a wife and seven children.

Project: For your eyes only

Many soldiers from all different countries carry good luck charms. Why do you think they carry them? Find out what sort of items they carried.

Make or draw a lucky charm to give to a soldier on the front-line.

West Africa 77

PEOPLE PROFILES Flying Officer John Henry Smythe OBE

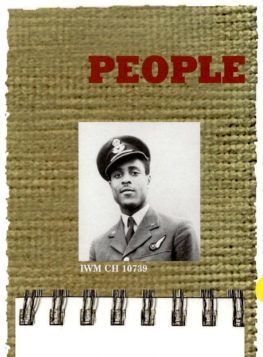

IWM CH 10739

FACT FILE
- **D.O.B** 30 June 1915
- **P.O.B** Freetown, Sierra Leone
- **D.O.D** 1996, Thame, England
- **Years of service**
  1941—1951 (RAF)
- **Rank** Flying Officer
- **Unit** No. 623 Squadron
- **Branch** Royal Air Force
- **Engagements**
  World War II
- **Awards** Member of the Order of British Empire (OBE)
- **Other Work**
  Sierra Leone Defence Force
  Administrator, Colonial Office
  Solicitor General of Sierra Leone

Johnny Smythe hated Hitler and everything he said and did.

He was disgusted when Hitler refused to shake hands with African American Jesse Owens when he won four gold medals at the 1936 Berlin Olympics— simply because he was black.

At the outbreak of war, Smythe volunteered to help in the war effort and joined the RAF in the UK, having already spent time serving with the Sierra Leone Defence Force.

He trained to become a navigator and was only one of four, out of 90 men in total to complete his training. He was then posted to a bomber squadron, which flew planes such as Lancaster bombers.

Flying missions into enemy airspace was always a dangerous job. Sometimes air crews did not return as they were hit by enemy fire, forcing them to crash-land, injuring or killing the occupants.

Several times Smythe found himself on board when his plane was attacked but he managed to escape injury— until the night of 18 November 1943 on his 28th mission.

> "We were flying at 16,000 feet when the fighters came out of nowhere. They raked the fuselage and there were flames everywhere. Then the searchlights caught us. I was hit by shrapnel. Pieces came from underneath, piercing my abdomen, going through my side. Another came through my seat and into my groin.
>
> I heard the pilot ordering us to bail out! We had some rough ones before but this seemed to be the end. I have tried to forget that night for 50 years."

Smythe jumped out of the plane, parachuted to the ground and hid in a barn.

Smythe being instructed in the use of the sextant (see page 94) IWM CH10740

78

The 1936 Olympic Games in Berlin was intended to showcase Nazi sporting prowess, which promoted the idea of Aryan racial superiority and Ethnic Africans were considered inferior. On the first day of the Games, Hitler shook hands only with German winners. Olympic committee officials insisted that he greet all medallists or none at all. Hitler chose not to greet any medallist. However the Games are better remembered for the sporting triumphs of black American sprinter Jesse Owens (pictured) who not only set an unofficial world record in the second heat of the 100 metre race, but went on to win four gold medals in both track and field events.
IWM HU63371

A course and speed calculator used by RAF navigators.
IWM AIR31

> "Men in uniform came into the barn where I was hiding behind some straw. Then they opened up, raking the place with automatic fire. I decided to give in. The Germans couldn't believe their eyes. I'm sure that's what saved me from being shot immediately. To see a black man – and an officer at that – was more than they could come to terms with. They just stood there gazing."

He was captured by German troops and taken to Stalag Luft 1, a POW camp in Pomerania. There were 9,000 other Allied troops imprisoned there. In 1945 he was freed by the Russians.

After the War, Smythe worked at the Colonial Office helping Commonwealth volunteers to return to their homelands. In 1948 he travelled with the *Empire Windrush* which carried 500 West Indian ex-servicemen and workers to the UK.

During this time he studied hard, passed his university exams and returned to Sierra Leone in 1951 where he practised law. Smythe eventually became the Solicitor General for his country. In 1978 he was awarded an OBE and in 1993 he returned to England with his wife and five children.

Johnny Smythe OBE died in Thame, Oxfordshire, England in 1996.

Stalag Luft I Prisoner of War Camp. IWM HU48923

Project: For your eyes only

COVER STORY.
You are an RAF navigational researcher. Before compasses and other navigational equipment were invented, people found their way using the natural environment. Investigate and write a report on the different ways you can navigate during daylight and in darkness using landmarks and the stars.

West Africa 79

SECTION 3

Unit 4: East Africa

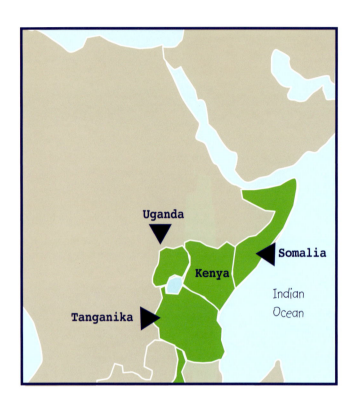

Abyssinian leader, Emperor Haile Selassie commanded his troops to fight against the attack and declared war on Italy. His army contained a massive 500,000 men but they were either new recruits or soldiers who were only experienced in fighting with bows and spears. The few rifles they had were old and unlikely to beat the Italians' modern weapons.
Despite this, the Abyssinians did the best they could and turned out to be fierce fighters, so the Italians fought back with poisonous gas. Mustard gas was dropped from Italian planes into towns and villages with deadly accuracy. Many Abyssinian soldiers and civilians were killed.

Emperor Selassie was removed from power and forced into exile. He fled to England. The Italians annexed Abyssinia on 9 May 1936. The new *Africa Orientale Italiana* or 'Italian East Africa' consisted of Abyssinia, Italian Somaliland and Eritrea.

Back in the 1880s, modern day Kenya, Uganda, Zanzibar and part of Tanzania, were all controlled by the British. At the same time the Germans had colonies in East Africa called *Deutsch Ostafrika* or 'German East Africa.' These areas are now Burundi, Rwanda and Tanzania. However Germany had to give up these colonies to Great Britain and Belgium after losing World War I.

In the 1880s Italy had one African colony in the north, Libya as well as Eritrea and Italian Somaliland in the east. In 1895 the Italians tried to take Abyssinia by force but were defeated a year later. In the mid 1930s, Italy's fascist leader, Mussolini wanted to increase his power base in Africa so he set up new colonies. Italy still possessed Italian Somaliland and Eritrea and Mussolini resumed Italy's claim on Abyssinia by sending in the military in October 1935.

Men of the King's African Rifles collecting surrendered arms after the last Italians had finally surrendered in Abyssinia, 1941.
IWM IWM E6064

80

Men of the Kenyan Royal Naval Volunteer Reserve operate a Lewis gun on board the minesweeper HMS ONYX, *while on a local river patrol.*

The Royal Naval Volunteer Reserve, Kenya, was formed in 1932 by a few local European residents, its main object being the naval side of local defence. Europeans in sufficient numbers were not obtainable locally, and it was decided to recruit from up-country. A Native Unit, part permanent, part volunteer, was also formed, and after much hard work, proved very useful. Duties carried out by the Force during the outbreak of war include minesweeping, coastal and inland water patrols, part Examination Service, Port War Signal Station, work in conjunction with the military during the Italian Campaign, and Base Personnel. A few ships with personnel have been loaned for duty with the Royal Navy. IWM/K2645

On 10 June 1940, when Italy declared war on the Allies, Great Britain immediately began to shore up its defences in East Africa. It had the support of troops from British Somaliland, British East Africa, India, South Africa, Northern and Southern Rhodesia, Nyasaland and British West Africa. There was even a small commando unit from British Palestine as well as several thousand Abyssinian *askaris* who had deserted Italian units.

On the Axis side were the Italians, Eritreans, Abyssinians and Somali Dubats as well as a small contingent of Germans. About 70% of the Italian troops consisted of local East African *askaris*. Great Britain feared an attack on its supply routes along the Red Sea and through the Suez Canal as well as on its colonies in Egypt and British Somaliland.

The King's African Rifles in Kenya. AWN 6182

Askari is an Arabic, Turkish, Somali, Persian, and Swahili word meaning soldier

FACT FILE
East Africa Campaign, part of the British Middle East Command
Dates
10 June 1940 — 27 November 1941
Battle locations
Sudan, British Somaliland, Kenya, Eritrea, Italian Somaliland, Abyssinia
Result
Allied Victory
Captured
230,000 Axis forces
Allied commanders
Field Marshal Sir Archibald Wavell
General Sir William Platt
General Sir Alan Cunningham
Emperor Haile Selassie

East Africa 81

After Italy's declaration of war, Commander-in-Chief of the British Middle East Command, Field Marshal Wavell needed more troops to assist as he was unsure where Italy would strike first and his troops were spread out across North and East Africa.

He called on Emperor Selassie for his support to rally local Abyssinian *askaris* who were still loyal, along with the British government who promised to help Selassie reclaim his throne from

Askaris of the 11th East African Division were later sent to Burma to support the war effort. IWM SE923

Emperor Haile Selassie with Brigadier D Sandford on his left and Major General O Wingate DSO on his right. IWM E2462

Two members of the 'Shifta' Abyssinian patriots, with rifles, in Kenya in 1941. IWM E1959

Abyssinian troops transporting supplies by camel through the bush in January 1941. IWM E1715

the Italians. Under the alias 'Mr Strong,' Emperor Selassie was flown from England to the Sudan in early July 1940 where he met Allied commander, General Platt, to discuss plans to free his country from Italian rule.

Another conference was held in October 1940 which was attended by Emperor Selassie, Field Marshal Jan Smuts, British Middle East military commanders and the British Foreign Secretary Anthony Eden. A general plan of attack was agreed which included using Abyssinian *askaris* who were still loyal to Selassie and FREEDOM FIGHTERS called 'Shiftas' who developed a resistance network against the Italians.

A month later, the British cracked the secret codes of the Italian Royal Army and Royal Air Force. From this point on, the Allied commanders knew about Italian plans as soon as they were issued. This was a major success for the Allies.

Another significant event was the formation of a special elite fighting unit called the Gideon Force, organised by Major General Orde Wingate DSO, who was later to create the Chindits in the Burma campaign (see page 44).

With the secret codes gathered from the code-breakers and highly skilled forces, the Allies were able to defeat the Italians. Emperor Selassie was returned to Abyssinia in January 1941 and he continued his reign until 1974. Other battles across the region raged on until the final surrender of the Italians in November 1941.

> **The UK's main decryption centre was at Bletchley Park, Buckinghamshire, and was known as Station X. Ciphers and codes from several Axis countries were decrypted here including the German Enigma and Lorenz machines.**

> "To raise a revolt you must send in a *Corps d'Elite* to do exploits and not just as peddlers of war, material and cash ... A thousand resolute and well-armed men can paralyse 10,000."
>
> *Major General Orde Wingate DSO*

SPECIAL UNIT

East Africa Gideon Force

Name	The Gideon Force
Branch	British SOE Force
Active	1940—1941
Engagements	East African Campaign
Commanders	Major General Orde Wingate DSO
	Emperor Haile Selassie

The Gideon Force was named by Wingate after the biblical figure Gideon, who defeated a large army with a small group of men. It was an elite army force of 50 officers, 20 British non-commissioned officers, a battalion from the Sudan Frontier Battalion and a battalion of Abyssinian *askaris*, the 2nd Ethiopian Battalion.

In total there were about 2,000 men along with 18,000 camels used for transport. Their key objective was to get Emperor Selassie back to Addis Ababa, along with supporting local resistance groups against the Italians. The force was officially broken up on 1 June 1941.

A Bren gun carrier ploughing its way through the shrubbery of a village in Eritrea. IWM E2184

Project: For your eyes only

COVER STORY. Operation Join Now
You are a recruiting officer in Africa.
Choose which region you want to recruit
from South Africa, Southern Africa,
West or East Africa.
Design an advertising campaign to
recruit Africans into the Army.
Would you use newspapers, radio,
cinema, posters or other media?

Design posters, radio and cinema ads, write a
newspaper article. How else could you reach them?
How would the campaign differ in each region?

Informal photograph of soldiers of the King's African Rifles. IWM E1968

East Africa 83

SECTION 4
West Indies

FACT FILE
1939 Population 14,000,000
Serving 10,000
Killed/missing in action 236
Wounded 265

A painting of a West Indian roadside scene.
IWM ART LD 3152

The West Indies consists of more than 7,000 islands, islets, reefs and cays situated in the Caribbean Sea and Atlantic Ocean. They are called the West Indies because when Christopher Columbus landed in 1492 he thought he had arrived in the Indies, or the islands southeast of India, by sailing westwards from Europe.

This area is now known as the Caribbean which comes from the word 'Carib' which was the name of one of the indigenous peoples who lived there; before and during European contact (see box on right). After the Europeans arrived many indigenous people were murdered for their land and possessions; others died from diseases such as smallpox and measles, to which they had no resistance.

The Europeans arrived in their thousands once they heard of the new lands to the west, which they called the 'New World'. The British, French, Spanish, Portuguese, Dutch, Swedish and Danish colonised the Caribbean islands, North and South America. They also fought among themselves over various islands.

In the 1640s Portuguese Jews emigrated from Brazil to Barbados, bringing with them the techniques to cultivate sugar-cane and establishing sugar-cane plantations. Huge numbers of people were required to work on the plantations to produce sugar for the European market. This was the start of the transatlantic slave trade.

Around 12 million enslaved men, women and children, mainly from West Africa, were taken to the Caribbean and forced to work on the plantations in appalling conditions. For the plantation owners, merchants, slave shippers and investors it was a highly lucrative industry.

However, many Europeans were alarmed at the conditions faced by African slaves and disturbed by the concept of enslaving fellow human beings. They pressured their governments to stop slavery in the colonies and the trading and shipping of people from Africa to the colonies.

Starting in 1803, Denmark abolished the slave trade, followed by the UK, France, Holland, Spain and finally Sweden in 1824. However, the trade continued until the late 1860s. From 1833 to 1880 slavery was abolished across most of the formally acknowledged colonies. The freeing of the slaves was called emancipation; the newly-freed received no compensation while their owners shared £20 million. After emancipation, people were still needed to work in the plantations so some of those freed from slave ships and a large number of people from India were exported to the British Caribbean colonies. The blending of Africans, Indians and Europeans led to the multicultural and multiracial make-up of the Caribbean.

The first colonies to gain independence were Haiti in 1804, the Dominican Republic in 1844 and Cuba in 1898. The first British colonies to gain independence were Jamaica and Trinidad & Tobago in 1962, followed by Guyana and Barbados in 1966, the Bahamas in 1973, Grenada in 1974, Dominica in 1978, St Lucia and St Vincent & the Grenadines in 1979, Antigua in 1980, Belize in 1981 and St Kitts & St Nevis in 1983.

British West Indies in 1939

- Barbados
- Bahamas
- Jamaica
- Cayman Islands
- Turks & Caicos Islands
- Trinidad & Tobago
- British Honduras (now Belize)
- British Guiana (now Guyana)
- British Windward Islands: Grenada, St Lucia, St Vincent, the Grenadines and Dominica
- British Leeward Islands: Antigua, Barbuda, British Virgin Islands, Montserrat, St Kitts, Nevis, Anguilla

INDIGENOUS PEOPLES OF THE CARIBBEAN

- Arawak
- Carib
- Ciguayo
- Garifun
- Lucayan
- Taino
- Kalinago
- Ciboney
- Galibi
- Igneri
- Macorix

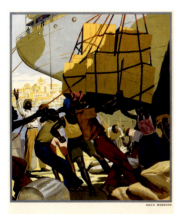
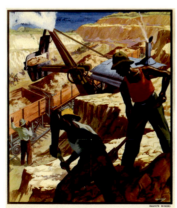

War posters designed to encourage civilians to contribute to the war effort. LtoR: IWM PST 8270, IWM PST 8271, IWM PST 8269, IWMPST 8238

Troops rushing from a carrier to take up position with a Bren gun.
IWM E31212

At the start of World War II many West Indians wanted to enlist in the British military. However the British War Office was reluctant to recruit black people from the colonies, despite the fact that West Indians had fought in World War I. Winston Churchill had sent a telegram to every Embassy and High Commission, telling them to find "administrative means" to reject black volunteers.

Eventually, due to the shortage of manpower and the fear of serious protests in the Carribean, some hundreds of well-qualified men were recruited as air crew and about 5,000 as ground crew for the RAF. Seventy became commissioned officers and over 100 were decorated for their bravery.

Many thousands of West Indians also served in merchant navy ships bringing food and raw materials to Britain. After much discussion between Caribbean leaders, the Colonial Office and the War Office, a special unit was raised in April 1944 — the Caribbean Regiment. A significant number of West Indians also enlisted in the Canadian and United States armed forces to get around the British colour bar.

If We Must Die

If we must die, let it not be like hogs
Hunted and penned in an inglorious spot,

While round us bark the mad and hungry dogs,
Making their mock at our accursed lot.

If we must die, O let us nobly die,
So that our precious blood may not be shed

In vain; then even the monsters we defy
Shall be constrained to honor us though dead!

O kinsmen we must meet the common foe!

Though far outnumbered let us show us brave,

And for their thousand blows deal one deathblow!

What though before us lies the open grave?

Like men we'll face the murderous, cowardly pack,

Pressed to the wall, dying, but fighting back!

Jamaican Poet, Claude McKay (1890-1948)

This poem was written by McKay in 1919 in New York when blacks were being attacked and lynched by white people across the USA. It became a popular poem of resistance. During his address to the American Congress in his effort to encourage American aid and American entry in the fight against German Nazism, Winston Churchill (pictured right) ended his speech by reading this poem. He also used it to rally the British people during the war. IWM HU55521

A recruit from the first contingent of ground staff volunteers for the Royal Air Force from the West Indies, holding his newly-issued kit in Bedfordshire, England.
IWM CH12148

Project: For your eyes only

 Why do you think that Churchill used McKay's poem to rally support from the USA and to motivate the British people?

Why would this poem appeal to Churchill?

SPECIAL UNITS

The Caribbean Regiment

Name	1st Battalion, Caribbean Regiment Carib Regiment
Branch	British Army
Active	1944—1946
Stationed	Middle East Italy Egypt

It was due to British reluctance that the regiment was not formed until April 1944. It had 1,200 volunteers from all over the West Indies and a few officers and NCOs were drafted in from British Army units.

The regiment trained first in Trinidad and then in Virginia, USA. It was then sent to Italy, and for intensive training in Palestine as there was resistance from Army authorities to use a West Indian regiment. It was then posted to Egypt to guard POWs and assist with mine clearance work. In 1946 the regiment returned to the West Indies and was disbanded.

A 2 inch mortar team ready for action.
IWM E31198

British Honduras Forestry Unit

A member of the British Honduras Forestry Unit carrying a tree trunk over his shoulder IWM D6395

Name	British Honduras Forestry Unit
Branch	Civilian Unit, Ministry of Supply
Active	1941—1943
Stationed	Scotland

In June 1941 the British government needed to increase the amount of timber that was produced within the UK. Civilian workers were brought in from Newfoundland, Eire and 500 skilled loggers from British Honduras. They were stationed in East Lothian, Berwickshire and Dumfriesshire in Scotland.

Accommodation had not been prepared for the men's arrival, neither had they been issued with appropriate clothing. When constructed, their living quarters were very poor and they had few recreational facilities. To add to their problems, the men's familiarity with cutting mahogany was not relevant to Scottish timber. They also found it difficult to adjust to the cold Scottish weather and faced discrimination from the locals.

By 1943 the Ministry of Supply wanted the West Indians repatriated due to their poor health, alleged inefficiency and 'associations' with white women in the area. The Colonial Office disagreed, finding that the West Indians didn't behave any worse than the other foreigners, but noted that because they were black they got more attention. They were also worried that if they returned the men to the Caribbean it could cause political unrest, as many West Indians were questioning the non-recruitment of Caribbean troops for the war effort, while others wanted equal rights and independence from Great Britain.

Nevertheless, the decision was made to send the men home in September 1943 but their travel arrangements were badly handled with some men being temporarily imprisoned on Ellis Island in the USA. Others stayed on in Great Britain but often faced discrimination when looking for work.

Merchant Navy and Royal Navy

West Indian ratings of the Trinidad Royal Naval Volunteer Reserve operating a depth-charge thrower. IWM K7524

Thousands of West Indian seamen made their contributions in one of WW II's most dangerous services, the Merchant Navy—one-third of all merchant seamen were killed during the war. The ships on which they worked were also targets for German submarines which hunted oil tankers, bauxite carriers and other cargo ships making their way to the USA and UK.

At the start of the War, thousands of black seaman who were resident in British port cities such as Liverpool, Cardiff, Glasgow and London offered to volunteer for the Merchant Navy, but their offers were turned down as the seamen's unions wouldn't allow blacks to apply to a ship where there was a white candidate for the job.

In the West Indies many men also volunteered their services including 300 applications from Antigua and 100 from St Lucia. Two St Lucians, Leo Bousquet and Marcus George, even wrote directly to the Minister of Shipping Sir John Gilmore in London. They reminded him of the many St Lucians who enlisted during World War I on the HMS *Good Hope* and who subsequently went down with the ship off the Falkland Islands. They even offered to donate £1 per month from their salary towards the Red Cross or other relief fund for the Navy.

The British government was in a difficult position. On the one hand the Colonial Office recognised there was a huge shortage of labour which could be filled by West Indians, but the Ministry of Shipping, ship owners and trade unions were reluctant to use West Indian labour.

By 1941 an agreement was reached and an employment pool was formed of West Indian seaman who could work on British ships. The British Sailors' Society provided and managed segregated hostels to accommodate them while they were in Great Britain.

Most of the merchant ships that West Indian men served on were old and slow. They worked below deck shovelling coal, and were paid less than white sailors for doing the same work.

> *"On all the oceans white caps flow you do not see crosses row on row, but those that sleep beneath the sea, rest in peace for your country is free"*
>
> Unknown

British Guiana Coastal Defence gun crew at practise.

British Guiana was the only British colony on the South American mainland. Lying just north of the equator and bounded by the Atlantic, Venezuela, Brazil and Dutch Guiana, it covers an area of just under 90,000 square miles. The population averaged less than four to a square mile but 90% of them live along a narrow, fertile strip of coastland where sugar and rice are cultivated.
British Guiana had important resources such as timber, as well as gold, diamonds, bauxite and other minerals. The population of the colony is made up mainly of people of African and Indian descent (37% and 43% respectively), with small numbers of Europeans, Chinese and aboriginal Amerindians. During the War large numbers of men volunteered for service with the British Guiana Battalion, others served with the Royal Air Force and the Merchant Navy or enlisted as tradesmen in the British Army.
IWM K10385

SPECIAL UNIT

Trinidad Royal Naval Volunteer Reserve

Name Trinidad Royal Naval Volunteer Reserve (TRNV)
Branch Royal Navy
Active 1939—1946

In the West Indies, the British Royal Navy formed the Trinidad Royal Naval Volunteer Reserve in 1939. It was administered by the local government and operated by the British Admiralty. Over 1,000 recruits came from all over the West Indies, with about half coming from Trinidad, the remainder from other islands.

Training included drill, learning how to tie knots, use a compass, handle small craft, signal, row, and specialised training in certain trades. When training was completed the men were transferred to minesweepers, motor launches, or given small harbour craft to handle. The role of the TRNV was to carry out patrols and distribute supplies around the West Indies.

Naval Police of the Trinidad Royal Naval Volunteer Reserve who guarded the gates of the naval base and other shore establishments. IWM K7530

Three West Indian merchant seaman are welcomed by the warden upon arrival at a hostel in Newcastle-Upon-Tyne. IWM D5762

German submarines patrolled the area attacking shipping. On the night of 9 March 1942 a German U-Boat, U161, launched a surprise attack on St. Lucia, which had both a US naval station and air base. U161 silently slipped into the shallow, tiny port of Castries in St Lucia and torpedoed two vessels in the harbour, a Canadian steamship the *Lady Nelson* and British freighter *Umtata*. The blast also caused damage to near-by houses. Fortunately a third vessel that was loaded with explosives escaped damage. There were 20 casualties and the crew members were housed locally.

To commemorate the incident a Caribbean calypso style song was created which ended with the words below:

> God bless *Lady Nelson*
> God bless de *Umtata*
> De submarine she come
> Right in de harbour
> Bomb *Lady Nelson*
> An' sink de *Umtata*

A tanker explodes after being torpedoed by a U-boat in the Caribbean. IWM MISC 51235

A German U-boat. IWM HU40215

West Indies **89**

West Indian Aid

The people of Jamaica supply a Crusader tank to Britain. IWM P1013

A mobile canteen bought by the people of British Honduras, being run and used by local citizens of Kendal. IWM ZZZ7104D

'Jamaica Hut' in Hampshire. IWM H37516

Aside from sending people to serve in the armed forces, many countries from the Empire contributed to the British war effort with cash and other resources.

While the West Indies was one of the smaller territories in the Empire they still sent aid. The government provided interest-free loans and ordinary people raised funds to support the was effort. By March 1943, the Trinadians alone had contributed more than £50,000.

As a small island nation, it was impossible for Great Britain to become self-reliant for food or the necessary war materials. For example, many millions of tons of bauxite were imported from British Guiana.

Human resources
Skilled tradesmen were in demand as there were severe labour shortages in factories across England, with British men being conscripted to fight in the war. However, only 520 workers were sent from the West Indies because of Government concerns that black men would not be accepted by the factories, they were housed in segregated hostels.

Military and civilian equipment
Jamaican newspaper '*The Gleaner*' launched a fundraising campaign '*Bombers for Britain*' to buy aircraft for Great Britain. Jamaica and many other colonies contributed to the campaign and 12 Blenheims were bought in 1941. Lord Beaverbrook, the wartime Minister of Aircraft Production, said in recognition of this astonishing effort, "Jamaica's name shall evermore be linked with a squadron of the Royal Air Force". The 139 Squadron, became known as 139 (Jamaica) Squadron. The people of the West Indies also supplied other

Jamaican technicians working at a tank factory. LtoR IWM D6211, IWM D6202

People of the West Indies gave funds to furnish recreation huts at Anti-Aircraft Command gun sites in Great Britain, where gunners and other personnel could take a break from duty. In acknowledgement of their contributions, the name of the island was permanently displayed on a plaque.
IWM ZZZ11482D

Learie Constantine, the famous cricketer from Trinidad who was employed as a Welfare Officer for West Indians working in Britain, introduces skilled engineers, boiler makers and motor mechanics from the West Indies to the Minister of Labour, Ernest Bevin. IWM SG8615C

Lord Moyne, Secretary of State for the Colonies, autographing the tail plane of an aircraft purchased by the people of Jamaica. IWM CH3579

military and civilian equipment such as Crusader tank and ambulances.

Mobile canteens
Mobile canteens were presented to the Ministry of Food by the people of the West Indies. They travelled to areas that had been affected by air attacks, feeding the homeless and also Civil Defence workers. The canteens were often operated by the Women's Voluntary Service.

Scrap metal
The West Indians collected scrap metal that would be re-used in Great Briain. From park railings to pots and pans, they sent any kind of metal that was no longer needed. Scrap metal was recycled and used in ammunitions, ships, tanks, aeroplanes, guns and shells.

Sanctuary
In 1940 Jamaica became a safehaven for around 1,500 civilian evacuees from Gibraltar, a British colony in the Mediterranean, along with several hundred Jewish European refugees. They were housed in what are now the grounds of the University of West Indies, but back then was known as Gibraltar Camp.

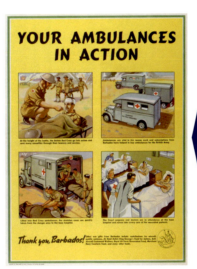

"At the height of the battle, the British Red Cross go into action and save many casualties through their bravery and service. Ambulances are vital to this rescue work and subscriptions from Barbados have helped to buy ambulances for the British Army..." This illustrated poster explains what the Barbados ambulances do and what other contributions Barbados has made to the British war effort.
IWM PROC 168

Project: For your eyes only

COVER Story. BritAid
You are living in the West Indies and want to help the war effort.
The Germans are causing major damage by bombing British cities. People have lost their homes and their lives.
Design a poster to raise money to help British families that are victims of the War.

West Indies **91**

In an attempt to upgrade the 'dowdy' image of the ATS, Abram Games designed the first of three recruiting posters in August 1941. The 'Blonde Bombshell', with its implications of potential sexual freedom within a more mobile female wartime population, was withdrawn from circulation by the government for being unsuitable.
IWM PST 2832

In April 1941 the ATS in Great Britain was given full military status although members were paid two-thirds of the wage of men of the same rank. In the same year the British government passed the National Service Act which permitted the conscription of women into war work or the armed forces.

Women of the ATS performed a wide variety of jobs such as drivers, ammunition inspectors, mess orderlies, mechanics and military police. They also played a large role in the Anti-Aircraft Command of the Royal Artillery, known as 'ack-ack'. They would find enemy aircraft, operate searchlights and control the direction of the gun, although officially they never fired them. ATS women were posted all over Great Britain and in most of the theatres of war.

More than 250,000 women served with the British ATS during World War II including Queen Elizabeth II, who served as Second Lieutenant Elizabeth Windsor, and Mary Churchill, the youngest daughter of the Prime Minister Winston Churchill.

HRH Princess Elizabeth, aka 2nd Lieutenant Elizabeth Windsor, wearing overalls and standing in front of a truck; behind her is a medical lorry.
IWM TR2835

SPECIAL UNIT

Auxiliary Territorial Service

Name   Auxiliary Territorial Service (ATS)
Branch   Attached to local West Indian battalions
Active   1943—1947

Many of the islands of the West Indies formed their own ATS which allowed women to enlist and to take an active role in the war effort. The majority of women stayed on the islands where they trained. They were issued army uniforms and had to learn army drills and discipline. Once trained, they were placed in administrative roles or had kitchen and mess hall duties at their local HQ offices. ATS personnel worked a minimum eight hours a day, were often not required to work weekends nor live in barracks. During the War 600 West Indian women volunteered for the ATS with half of them serving overseas – 200 in the USA and 100 in Great Britain.

The ATS was modelled on the British Auxiliary Territorial Service (see left) which had been formed in 1938 and was, based and organised in the same way as the Territorial Army. The new ATS included members of the First Aid Nursing Yeomanry (FANY), one of the first women's voluntary corps, which had been highly valued during World War I.

A group of ATS clerks at work in the storeroom of the Trinidad Base Command, Port of Spain, Trinidad in 1945. IWM K8832

Inspection Parade of ATS Members in November 1944 at St James' Barracks, Port of Spain, Trinidad. IWM K8831

Women of Jamaica's first ATS unit in 1944 IWM K5926

A number of ATS volunteers from the West Indies, who were based in one of Britain's Ordnance Depots, attend a garden party given in their honour by members of the Women's Voluntary Services and British Legion Women's Section at Bicester. Pte. Jackman from Barbados receives a rose from her hostess, Mrs Coker. IWM D21328

ATS Marching Song

Do you know of a little island
Where the sea is so blue
And the girls of this island
Have turned to something new
They have shed their pretty pretties
And donned the Uniform
Because their King and Country called them to help weather
the storm

It's only a little island
But it's heart is full of gold
It's only a little Island
But the girls they have been told
So they came and joined the Army
And drilled upon the square
And now they're every bit the soldier
But for their skirts and hair

But what does all this matter
When all is said and done
For they work without chatter
And their work is just begun
They will serve without flinching to the bitter end
For they know that you are returning
To wife and child and friend

Written by Colonel K G G Denys, and dedicated to the women of the ATS of St Lucia.

An ATS leather jerkin issued to Anti-Aircraft Gun site personnel. IWM UNI 11005

Project: For your eyes only

COVER STORY: Operation Join Now
You are a recruiting officer for the ATS in the West Indies. Design an advertising campaign to recruit women into the ATS. What would be the best way to reach them? Would you use newspapers, radio, cinema, posters or other media? Design posters, radio and cinema ads, write a newspaper article. How else could you reach them?

West Indies

SPECIAL UNIT

ROYAL AIR FORCE

Leading Aircraftwoman Lilian Bader was born in Liverpool to a Barbadian father and English mother, but was orphaned by the age of nine and grew up in a convent. At the start of the war she joined the Navy, Army and Air Force Institutes (NAAFI) but was later rejected because her father had not been born in the UK.

She heard that the RAF accepted coloured people, so joined the Women's Auxiliary Air Force (WAAF) in 1941 and soon attained the rank of acting corporal. She was one of the first women in the WAAF to be trained as an instrument repairer, which had been a man's skill so the men could be released for overseas duties.
IWM HU53753

A contingent of 1,000 volunteers for the RAF on the deck of their troop ship, shortly after its arrival at Liverpool, England.
IWM CH3438

A sextant is a navigational instrument which was used by RAF navigators to calculate latitude and longitude. IWM AIR 322

The West Indies' most visible achievement during World War II was their contribution to the Royal Air Force. In 1940 the Air Ministry advised the Colonial Office that it would accept qualified air crew volunteers and men with training in a trade from the colonies.

The first group of recruits trained in Canada with the Royal Canadian Air Force's Initial Training Wings. They were then granted commissions and according to the Under Secretary of State for the Dominions "were treated in all respects as if they were white."

FAMOUS WEST INDIAN RAF CREW

Arthur Wint (Jamaican Olympic Gold Medallist & High Commissioner)

Edward Dalrymple aka Dr Scobie (Vice-President of Dominican Freedom Party and Professor Emeritus, New York University)

Michael Manley (Prime Minister of Jamaica)

Errol Barrow (Prime Minister of Barbados)

The RAF is often considered the elite of the armed forces with fighter pilots and bombing crews often portrayed as white and upper class. Yet around 500 West Indians served as air crew with a further 5,500 – 6,000 serving as ground crew.

Lincoln Orville Lynch DFM, an air gunner serving with No. 102 Squadron, Royal Air Force, photographed wearing his flying kit by the rear turret of a Handley Page Halifax at Pocklington, Lincolnshire. Lynch, from Jamaica, volunteered for service in the RAF in 1942, and in 1943 won the Air Gunner's trophy for obtaining the highest percentage in his course during training in Canada. On his first operational flight with No. 102 Squadron he shot down a German Junkers Ju 88. IWM CH12263

A O Weekes of Barbados and Flight Sergeant C A Joseph of Trinidad of the No. 122 (Bombay) Squadron.
IWM CH11478

This blue serge single-breasted four- pocket RAF service dress jacket belonged to Cpl. Euton George Christian from Jamaica. He joined the RAF when he was 21. On either sleeve, below the Royal Air Force Eagle badge, are sewn the rank stripes of a Corporal. Above the left breast pocket are undress ribbons for the Defence Medal 1939-45 and the War Medal 1939-45. IWM UNI 11593

PEOPLE PROFILE Flight Lieutenant the Rt. Hon. Dudley Thompson
OJ, QC, MA (OXON)

FACT FILE
D.O.B 19 January 1917
P.O.B Panama
Years of Service
   1941—1945
Rank Flight Lieutenant
Unit 49 Pathfinders Squadron
Branch Royal Air Force (RAF)
Engagements
   World War II
Awards Order of Jamaica (OJ)
   Order of Balboa (Panama)
   Mico Gold Medalist (Teaching, Jamaica)
   Living Legend of Africa 2006 (Ghana)
Other Work
   Lawyer
   Pan-African Activist
   Politician
   Ambassador
   Statesman
   Author

Born in Panama and raised in Jamaica, Dudley Thompson started his career as a teacher.

He had been awarded a government scholarship to attend Mico Training College. One day in 1940 while sitting in his dentist's waiting room, he picked up a magazine which had extracts of Adolf Hitler's book 'Mein Kampf'. As he read, Thompson became angered by the German leader's views on 'Negroes'. (see page 102) He felt that he had to fly to Germany and teach the Führer a lesson in manners.

Initially Thompson took a ship to Canada to train as a pilot. However the authorities advised him it would take two years of training before he could qualify as a pilot. Thompson couldn't wait that long, so he decided to travel to England instead.

On arriving in Great Britain, Thompson was accepted by the RAF and trained at the Officer's Training College at Cranwell. He served as a bomb aimer with the 49 Pathfinders Squadron and was awarded several decorations.

Towards the end of the war from 1944 to 1945 Thompson served as Jamaican liaison officer to the Colonial Office, where he assisted Jamaican ex-servicemen who wanted to settle in London.

After the war he attended Oxford University as a Rhodes Scholar and graduated with a Masters degree in Law, going on to become a barrister and relocating to East Africa.

In 1953, during the Mau Mau trials, Thompson was part of the international team defending Jomo Kenyatta, who was later to become Kenya's first indigenous Prime Minister and President.

Thompson returned to the West Indies, where he continued to practise law. He eventually became a government minister in Jamaica alongside a fellow RAF veteran, the then Jamaican Prime Minister Michael Manley.

He also served as Jamaica's Ambassador to Nigeria, Ghana and other African countries. He was awarded one of Jamaica's most prestigious decorations, the Order of Jamaica, for distinguished service in the field of International Affairs and for his contribution to legal developments in Jamaica.

In 2006 he was presented with the 'Living Legend' Award by African media in Ghana and in 2008 he became the President of the World Africa Diaspora Union.

The Rt. Hon. Dudley J Thompson, and his wife Cecile Eistrup have four daughters, a son, five grandchildren and one great-granddaughter.

West Indies 95

PEOPLE PROFILE
Flight Lieutenant Cy Grant

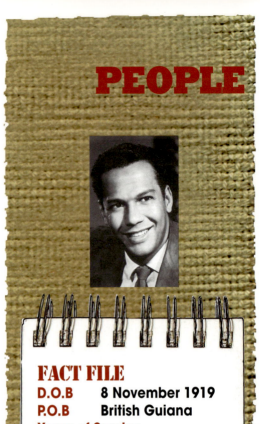

FACT FILE
- **D.O.B** 8 November 1919
- **P.O.B** British Guiana
- **Years of Service** 1941—1945
- **Rank** Flight Lieutenant
- **Branch** Royal Air Force (RAF)
- **Engagements** World War II
- **Awards** Honorary Fellow University of Surrey
- **Other Work**
    - Barrister
    - Author
    - Chairman/co-founder of Drum Arts Centre
    - Director of Concord Multicultural Arts
    - Singer
    - Broadcaster

Cy Grant moved from British Guiana to the UK to join the RAF, after it had removed its bar and allowed blacks from the colonies to join its ranks.

By 1943 Grant had received a commission and was one of the few black officers in the RAF. March 1943 was the start of the Battle of the Ruhr and whilst he was on his third mission, Grant's Lancaster Bomber was shot down over Holland on its return to England.

He managed to bail out, escaping serious injury, and landed in a field. A local farmer took him to his farm and gave him a hot meal. A local policeman was informed of Grant's presence and handed him over to the Germans. He was taken to an interrogation camp in Amsterdam before being transported with other POWs to Stalag Luft III. Later he was sent to another compound for officers a few miles away.

For Grant, the worst part of his imprisonment were the final months of the war, as the Russian army advanced and the Germans evacuated the camp. Grant and his fellow prisoners were forced to march in deep snow, with restricted rations, sleeping in barns and later being transported in cattle trucks to Lukenwalde, just south of Berlin. By the end of the War, they were freed by the Russians who ripped down the prison camp fences with their tanks.

After the War Grant studied law and qualified as a barrister but went on to become an actor and entertainer. In the 1970s he founded Drum, the London based, black arts centre, and was the director of the Concord Multicultural Festivals in the 1980s.

An aerial photograph taking during a daylight raid on an oil refinery in the Ruhr. IWM C4713

Stalag Luft III prisoner of war camp, scene of the 'Great Escape' in 1944. IWM HU21013

BATTLE OF THE RUHR

The Battle of the Ruhr was a five-month-long campaign of strategic bombing of a major industrial area of Germany called the Ruhr. The targets included armament factories, synthetic oil plants, coke plants, steelworks and dams.

Operation Chastise was part of this battle and was the official name for attacks on Germans dams on 16—17 May 1943. The RAF Squadron that carried out the attacks were known as the 'Dambusters' and they used specially developed 'bouncing bombs.'

Operation Chastise: the attack on the Moehne, Eder and Sorpe Dams by No. 617 Squadron RAF on the night of 16—17 May 1943. No. 617 Squadron practice dropping the 'Upkeep' weapon at Reculver bombing range, Kent. Here the bomb rises from the water after its first 'bounce'.
IWM FLM2342

Cy Grant a publisher of books, papers and poems, currently lives in North London. He wrote his war memoirs in 2006. Cy Grant was the first black person to appear regularly on British television with appearances on BBC's *Tonight* programme in the 1950s singing the news in calypso, and BBC's sci-fi show *Blake's 7* in the 1970s. He also provided the voice of Lieutenant Green in Gerry Anderson's *Captain Scarlet and the Mysterons*.

The RT Hon Colonel Oliver Stanley MC, MP (Secretary of State for the Colonies) and Air Marshal Sir Arthur Barratt, KCB, (Air Officer Commanding in Chief Technical Training Command) inspect new West Indian recruits to the RAF. Thousands of West Indian volunteers were trained and employed as ground crew.
IWM D_021133

Cy Grant published his memoirs under the title '*A Member of the RAF of Indeterminate Race*'*. The title is derived from a caption below a picture of him in a German Newspaper in July 1943 "*Ein Mitglied der Royal Air Force von unbestimmbarer Rasse!*" This was shown as propaganda for the German war machine, implying that the RAF had to resort to recruiting people of an unknown race to fight their wars for them.

**Published by Woodfield Publishing (2007)*

Dutch author Hans Klootwijk's book '*Lancaster W4827: Failed to Return*' tells the story of Cy Grant and his crew after their plane was shot down over Holland. The book is based on research carried out by Hans' father 'Joost' who was just 11 years old when the bomber crashed into a farmhouse in his village.

Klootwijk and Grant have since teamed up and created a website dedicated to the Caribbean aircrew who served in WWII at www.caribbeanaircrew-ww2.com

West Indies 97

PEOPLE PROFILE
Squadron Leader Philip Louis Ulric Cross
The Caribbean's Most Highly Decorated RAF Officer

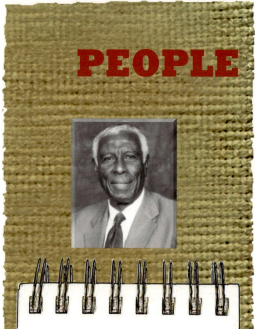

FACT FILE

- **D.O.B** May 1917
- **P.O.B** Port of Spain, Trinidad
- **Years of Service** 1941–1947
- **Rank** Squadron Leader
- **Unit** 139 (Jamaica) Squadron Bomber Command
- **Branch** Royal Air Force (RAF)
- **Engagements** World War II
- **Awards**
  - Distinguished Service Order (DSO)
  - Distinguished Flying Cross (DFC)
  - Order of Merit - First Class, Federal Republic of Cameroon
- **Other Work**
  - Ambassador
  - High Commisioner
  - High Court and Appeal Court Judge
  - Attorney General

In 1941 Ulric Cross decided to volunteer for the RAF as he saw that Dunkirk had been a bitter defeat for the British and that Nazis were gaining power across Europe.

Along with 250 other Trinidadians, he sailed for 12 days across the Atlantic Ocean to Great Britain. He trained at Cranwell, learning wireless operation, meteorology, bomb aiming, navigation and Morse code.

After graduating as a pilot officer he was assigned to Bomber Command, serving as a navigator in the 139 (Jamaica) Squadron.

Initially, Cross flew on several low-level daylight bombing missions in a very fast, small plyboard, two-man bomber planes called the Mosquito. They would fly at just 50 feet and drop four 500lb bombs.

The RAF discovered that only 20% of the bombs hit their targets so they set up a new group called the Pathfinder Force to guide the bombs. Cross joined this group. They dropped flares over the target and bombers following behind then bombed the flares.

Cross did 80 operational flights over Germany and occupied France, including 21 to Berlin. His planes didn't have guns: instead they used accurate navigation and speed to avoid enemy fire called 'flak'.

While most of his missions were successful, Cross and his pilot nearly died when they crash-landed after enemy flak destroyed one of the plane's engines. They couldn't make it to their RAF base at Witton so he had to work out a course to a closer one in Swanton Morley.

The base wasn't expecting them and Cross couldn't communicate with them because they had to maintain radio silence, otherwise the Germans would have been able to locate them. They had to land in complete darkness, and ended up overshooting the runaway and landing instead in a disused quarry.

98 .--. .-. --- ...- .. -.-. ...

Luckily their landing speed was slow and although they hit their heads badly, both survived. In fact Cross's only other injury during the War was to his knee when playing football in the snow!

Squadron Leader Cross was awarded the DFC in 1944 for his gallantry in the bombing attacks across occupied Europe. In 1945 he was also awarded the DSO in recognition of his "fine example of keenness and devotion to duty" and "exceptional navigational ability".

In 1949 he qualified as a lawyer, later serving as a judge in several African countries including Ghana, Cameroon, Tanzania as well as his home island of Trinidad.

He was also Trinidad's High Commissioner to the UK and an ambassador to Germany, France and Norway.

In 2002 author Ken Follett inspired by Ulric Cross, created a black Squadron Leader Charles Ford, in the prologue of his book, *Hornet Flight*.

Whilst the book was a success, a veteran RAF pilot from Zimbabwe was outraged that Follett had included a black Squadron Leader. In a letter to Follett, Alan Frampton, who served between 1942—1946 said:

"For the life of me, I cannot recall ever encountering a black airman of any rank whatsoever during the whole of my service."

Frampton believed that the author had included the character as a 'sop' or concession to black people.
He went on to say that:

"He (the author) aroused my indignation, remembering as I do, the real heroes of that period in our history, who were not black."

At the time Cross commented that he didn't understand how Frampton didn't know about him and other black members of the RAF and said, "I am old enough to have a certain amount of tolerance. People believe what they need to believe... When you know what you have done, what people think is irrelevant."

Distinguished Service Order and Distinguished Flying Cross.
IWM AIR 75_002

Project: For your eyes only

Why do you think RAF veteran Alan Frampton from Zimbabwe was so upset about the character Charles Ford in the book *Hornet Flight*?

Why do you think he never saw any black airmen during his service?
Write a letter to your local newspaper explaining the role that black airmen played in WWII.

West Indies

SECTION 5
Canada

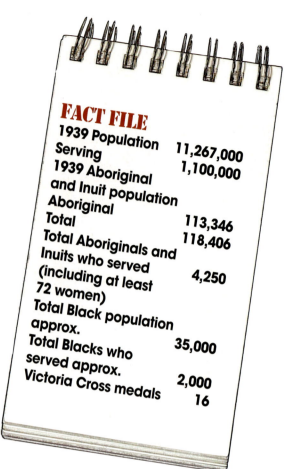

FACT FILE
1939 Population Serving	11,267,000
1939 Aboriginal and Inuit population	1,100,000
Aboriginal Total	113,346
Total Aboriginals and Inuits who served (including at least 72 women)	118,406
	4,250
Total Black population approx.	35,000
Total Blacks who served approx.	2,000
Victoria Cross medals	16

Canada is the second largest country in the world in land area. It has the longest coastline of any country in the world. It is bordered by the Pacific, Arctic and Atlantic oceans.

The indigenous peoples of Canada are believed to have first arrived between 40,000 and 16,500 years ago by crossing over the Bering Strait by a land bridge formed between Asia and Alaska during the last Ice Age. The first Europeans on Canadian soil were the Norse who landed in Newfoundland but only remained for a few years.

The British were the first to explore Canada's eastern coast in 1497 followed shortly by the French. By the early 17th century both the British and French had settled in various parts of the country. The French founded Quebec and Montreal and called the colony 'New France'.

French missionaries tried to convert the indigenous people to Christianity with little success and the settlers traded with them in furs and skins. However the settlers also passed on diseases to which they had no resistance. The introduction of guns and alcohol also had a negative impact on aboriginal communities.

In 1670 the English established the Hudson Bay Company which had exclusive right to trade with the locals for skins and furs. Rivalries between British and French settlers and traders caused many conflicts. There were also conflicts between indigenous groupings for control of trade and access to the European traders.

By 1763 the French were forced to surrender all their Canadian territories to Britain in the Treaty of Paris. The British enacted the Quebec Act of 1774 which allowed the French Canadians to practice their own religion— they were Roman Catholics— keep their language and to also keep French civil law alongside British criminal law. During this time black people also arrived in Canada. Some were slaves of European settlers and others were Loyalists who had supported the British during the American Revolution. The Loyalists were promised land and went on to found settlements in Nova Scotia and Ontario.

100

Contact with Europeans occurred at many different times for the aboriginal peoples of Canada. Some tribes came into contact with Europeans over 900 years ago, whilst the peoples of the north Atlantic met Europeans in the last 400 years. Other tribes such as the Inuit of Pond Inlet and Dene did not meet Europeans until the early 1900s.

Several times, armies from the United States of America tried to conquer Canada and take it from the British, but each time they were defeated. Canada became an independent country at Confederation in 1867 and was known as the Dominion of Canada. A railway was built and finished in 1885 which made travel easier and many Europeans moved to the west of the county and settled there.

Canadian soldiers including 4,000 indigenous and 1,000 of black heritage fought in World War I. In fact more Canadians died in this war, (over 70,000) than any other war. Women were given the right to vote by the end of the War. In 1931 the Statute of Westminster was passed which gave Canada absolute control over her own affairs.

On 10 September 1939 Canada declared war on Germany and played an important role in the D-Day Landings in 1944 and in liberating the Netherlands. Compulsory service or conscription was instituted in June 1940 which included peoples of the First Nation but not the Inuit (see page 102). In 1949, Newfoundland and Labrador became a part of Canada and a new flag was designed in 1965 — the Maple Leaf.

BEOTHUK

The Algonquian-speaking Beothuk were a semi-nomadic tribe who reached Newfoundland around 200AD. They were the first indigenous North American who came in to contact with British explorers who described them as 'Red Indians', as they covered themselves with red ochre. The last of the Beothuks were wiped out by 1829 from a combination of European diseases to which they had no resistance, such as small pox and measles, and constant fighting with the British settlers.

This drawing from 1619 shows four indigenous people of New France (Canada) from a book by Samuel de Champlain called 'Voyages et descouvertures faites en la Nouvelle France' or 'Travel and discoveries found in New France.' The two men at top are warriors armed with shields, bows and arrows; bottom left is a mother holding a paddle and nursing her infant; bottom right is a man dressed for winter wearing snowshoes.
USLC

The Canadian flag.

Canoes, toboggans and snowshoes are aboriginal technologies.

WHY DID THEY FIGHT?

- **Loyalty**
  To the British Crown – in the past Aboriginals primarily sided with the British against the French and Americans
- **Tradition**
  Many had relatives and who had served in World War I
- **Bravery**
  To prove they will still warriors
- **Money**
  To earn a regular wage
- **Civil rights**
  To gain equal rights
- **Comraderie**
  Their friends were also enlisting in the Forces
- **Conscription**
  Between 1943 and 1944

In Canada, **'Indians'** are known as **'Aboriginal Peoples'**, **'Native People'**, or **'People of the First Nations'**.

Inuit means **'the people'**. They were previously known as Eskimoes by Europeans.

Eskimo is a derogatory word and in Algonquian means raw meat eaters.

Métis are people who have dual European and Aboriginal heritage.

Negro means someone of black African ancestry. It was a neutral, formal term used up until 1960s. The word fell out of favour during the American Civil Rights movement, with leaders preferring words such as 'black,' ' black African' or 'African American'.

Over a million Canadians served in World War II. By 1943 conscription was introduced for all able men of military age for service in Canada and overseas; only the Inuit were exempt.

Many First Nations communities protested against conscription as they had been told during previous treaty negotiations that they wouldn't be caught up in British battles. They received an exemption in 1944. Despite this many Aboriginal peoples still volunteered, both for home defence and service abroad.

Like other parts of the Commonwealth, the Royal Canadian Air Force (RCAF) initially had a colour bar, so the majority of blacks and aboriginals enlisted in the army. In 1942 the 421 (Fighter) Squadron was formed which had a significant number of Aboriginal pilots and was nicknamed the 'Red Indian Squadron'.

Aboriginal and black women also played their part in the war. Many collected clothing and money for the British War Victim Fund, Red Cross and Salvation Army. They also worked alongside men in Canada's mammoth war industries.

While German and Japanese submarines posed a threat to Canadian waterways and coastlines, the country was safe from aerial bombardment. As a result Canadians were able to make and supply ammunitions, weapons, explosives, military vehicles, tanks, armoured gun carriers, aircraft, ships, radar sets and electronics which they sent to Great Britain, United States, Russia and other Allied countries.

Like the Australian Aboriginals, Canadian Aboriginals could not vote and were not full citizens of Canada. They were granted the right to vote in 1960.

Project: For your eyes only

Investigate the history of the indigenous peoples of Canada.

In what way are their experiences with European settlers, both past and present, similar to those faced by Australian Aboriginals and Islanders?

SPECIAL UNIT

1st Special Service Force

V42 Combat Knife.

The M1941 Johnson Light Machine Gun was an American recoil-operated, light machine gun.

Name	1st Special Service Force (1st SSF)
Call Sign	The Devils Brigade *die schwarzen Teufeln* (the Black Devils)
Branch	American Canadian Commando Unit
Active	1942—1944
Engagements	Italy France Aleutian Islands
Commander	Major General Robert T. Frederick (USA)

Scientist Geoffrey Pyke of the British Combined Operations Command hatched a plan to create a small elite military force that could fight behind enemy lines in winter conditions. Its mission would be to sabotage hydro electric plants and oil fields in occupied Norway, Romania and the Italian Alps. He also came up with an idea to develop a special vehicle that could carry men and equipment at high speed across snow and ice-covered terrain. Pyke called his idea 'Project Plough'.

Project Plough was given to the Americans at a conference in March 1942 as Great Britain didn't have the resources required to put the project into action. The Americans took the project on and asked car manufacturers to develop a design for a snowmobile. Studebaker then created the T-15 cargo carrier which later became known as the M29 Weasel.

Initially the unit was to be made up of equal numbers of American, Canadian and Norwegian troops but due a lack of Norwegians, the unit was changed to just Americans and Canadians.

Unit members were trained in stealth tactics, hand-to-hand combat, parachuting, ski warfare, mountain warfare and rock climbing. They were also issued equipment specifically for alpine and winter combat such as skis, parkas, haversacks and mountain rations. Troops were armed with the V-42 combat knife and M1941 Johnson machine gun.

Troops covered their faces in black boot polish when they worked in the cover of darkness. They would stealthily overpower the enemy without firing a shot and silently disappear back into the night. The 1SSF's call sign came about after troops found a diary of a German officer in which he referred to them as 'die schwarzen Teufeln', meaning "the Black Devils".

They also used to leave calling cards – stickers which they would place on enemy corpses and encampments with the slogan written in German *"Das dicke Ende kommt noch"* meaning "The worst is yet to come".

The unit disbanded on 5 December 1944 in southern France; the American troops honoured the Canadians with a marchpast, eyes right, officers saluting them.

The skills, tactics and strategies learned from the Devil Brigade's missions were used to create future elite units including the American Green Berets and Delta Force and Canada's JTF2 military unit.

Before World War II Canadian women were only allowed to be affiliated with the Canadian Army Medical Corp as nurses or members of the Red Cross, but officially they were not classed as members of the Canadian armed forces.

At the beginning of the War, women were keen to serve their country and support the troops. They set up the Women's Service Corps which was organised in a similar way to the men's armed forces. Their members were trained in drill and non-combat duties such as first aid, mechanical repairs and communications. At first both the government and military refused to have women serve in the armed forces. But, by 1941, there was such a huge labour shortage that the government changed its policy and the military created women's divisions. During the War some 50,000 women served their country directly in the armed forces.

Among these women of European heritage, a number of indigenous and black women also served. However, at enlistment, the records did not note people's ethnic heritage, so the exact number of serving indigenous and black women is not known.

One of the first indigenous women to join the CWAC was Private Mary Greyeyes who was sent to England to work in the Laundry Unit, as a cook. Private Greyeyes was from the Muskeg Lake Indian Reserve in Saskatchewan.

CWACs on their way to Italy.

SPECIAL WOMEN'S

Canadian Women's Army Corps (CWAC)

Branch	Canadian Army
Active	1941—964
Engagements	USA
	UK
	Italy
	Germany
	Northwest Europe
Commander	Colonel Elizabeth Smellie

Formed in 1941 the CWAC allowed women to take non-combat roles to free up men. CWAC members worked as secretaries, clerks, canteen workers, vehicle drivers, engineers, signallers and other non-combat military jobs such as logistics and planning. Members served both in Canada and overseas usually in military headquarter establishments.

Women were paid the equivalent of two-thirds of a serviceman pay and they couldn't claim any benefits for dependents, unlike the men. This was rectified by the government who increased their pay to four-fifths of their male counterparts and paid them benefits for parents and siblings but not for dependent spouses and children. This was an improvement on women working in the private sector who were still paid significantly less than men.

Over 21,000 women served during the war, with 3,000 being stationed in Europe as support staff for Canadian forces.

The CWAC was disbanded in 1964 when women were incorporated into the Canadian armed forces.

UNITS

Royal Canadian Air Force Women's Division (RCAFWD)

Branch   Royal Canadian Air Force
Active   1941—1946

Many members served at British Commonwealth Air Training Plan bases and schools as nursing assistants, cooks, stores women and clerks. They also took on jobs that had traditionally been performed by men such as drivers, vehicle mechanics, armourers, instrument makers, aircraft technicians, electricians and signalers. Some were sent to serve overseas in supporting roles.

After the service disbanded in 1946, women were allowed to join the Royal Canadian Air Force in 1951 and by 1988 Canada was the first western country to allow female pilots to fly fighter jets.

Women's Royal Canadian Naval Service (WRCNS)

Call Sign   Wrens
Branch   Royal Canadian Naval Service
Active   1942—1946

The Wrens were the smallest of the three women's divisions.

Enlisted members worked primarily in communications as signallers, wireless operators, telegraph operators, coders, and technicians.

The British Commonwealth Air Training Plan was an agreement between Canada, the United Kingdom, New Zealand and Australia to provide air-force training in Canada.

Canada was chosen because it had the space and training fields, was close to Great Britian but far away from enemy aerial bombardment. The agreement also allowed Commonwealth allies to share their air power resources. The Plan trained over 130,000 airmen.

Project: For your eyes only

COVER STORY. Operation Join Now
You are a recruiting officer for the Canadian Armed Forces.
Design an advertising campaign to recruit indigenous and black women into the Army, Navy or Air Force.
What would be the best way to reach them?
Would you use newspapers, radio, cinema, posters or other media?
Design posters, radio and cinema ads, write a newspaper article.
How else could you reach them?

Canada 105

PEOPLE PROFILE Brigadier Oliver Milton Martin

Canada's highest-ranking Aboriginal officer ever

Oliver Milton Martin was born a Mohawk from the Six Nations Grand River Reserve.

He trained to be a teacher but joined a volunteer army regiment called the Haldimand Rifles in 1909.

By 1915, along with this two brothers, he enlisted in the regular army. He spent several months in France and Belgium fighting with the Allies in WWI.

In 1917 he joined the Royal Air Force and qualified a year later as a pilot. After the War he left the armed forces, returned to Canada and became a school headmaster. However he remained with the Haldimand Rifles and became their commander in 1930.

At the start of World War II Martin trained hundreds of recruits at the Niagra-on-the-Lake training camp. Twelve months later he was promoted to the rank of brigadier, the first indigenous Canadian to achieve this rank. He commanded two infantry battalions.

Martin retired from active service in October 1944 and was awarded the Colonial Auxiliary Forces Officer's Decoration for his 20 years of service with good conduct.

Martin was held in high esteem and so widely respected that, after leaving the armed forces, he was appointed as a magistrate for the Ontario District, making him the first indigenous Canadian to hold a judicial post in Ontario. Brigadier Martin died in 1957.

TRIBUTES

Brigadier Martin and his wife were invited and attended the coronation of Queen Elizabeth II in 1953.

The East York branch of the Royal Canadian Legion is named the Brigadier O Martin Branch. Brigadier Martin was also inducted into the Canadian Indian Hall of Fame.

FACT FILE
- **D.O.B** 9 April 1893
- **P.O.B** Ohsweken, Ontario
- **D.O.D** 1957
- **Tribe** Mohawk
- **Years of Service** 1909—1944
- **Rank** Brigadier
- **Unit** Haldimand Rifles
   114th & 107th Battalions
   Royal Air Force
   13th Infantry Brigade
   14th (Nanaimo) Infantry Brigade
   16th (Prince George) Infantry Brigade
- **Engagements**
   World War I
   World War II
- **Awards** Colonial Auxiliary Forces Officer's Decoration
- **Other Work**
   Schoolteacher
   Headmaster
   Magistrate

Project: For your eyes only

COVER STORY. You are a newly enlisted private and are training at the Niagra-on-the-Lake under Brigadier Martin. This is your first time away from home. Write a letter to your family telling them about your experiences and how happy you are that your commander is also a fellow Mohawk.

PEOPLE PROFILE Flying Officer Gerald 'Gerry' Bell

Canada's first black airman

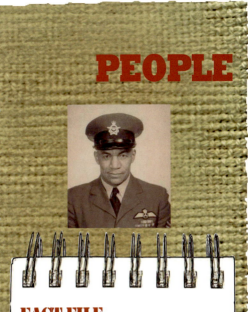

FACT FILE
D.O.B. 17 February 1909
P.O.B. Hamilton, Ontario
D.O.D. 17 January 1989
Years of Service
    1936—1961
Rank Brigadier
Unit 119th Bomber
    Reserve
    6th Bomber Group
    424th Squadron
    Branch
Branch Royal Canadian
    Air Force (RCAF)
Engagements
    World War II
Other Work
    Athlete
    Boxer
    Special Constable,
    Royal Canadian
    Mounted Police
    (RCMP)
    Military Quality
    Control Officer

Gerry Bell was born and raised in Hamilton, Canada.

While he studied medicine Bell served as a special constable and trained as an athlete, even competing against Olympic gold medallist Jesse Owens (see page 79).

One day Bell came across a pilot and plane at a local airstrip which inspired his lifelong passion for flying. He secretly took flying lessons—because he felt his parents wouldn't approve. However a local newspaper revealed his secret when they published an article about him called *The Brown Birdman* and *Canada's only Negro Aviator*.

After getting his pilot's licence Bell joined the RCAF but left shortly afterwards. In the meantime he continued with his athletics but suffered injuries that prevented him from competing in the Berlin Olympics of 1936; instead he attended as a trainer. After Berlin he rejoined the RCAF and served with the 119th Bomber Reserve in Hamilton.

At the start of the War Bell was sent to Britain where he trained the pilots of the 6th Bomber Group and served as an air gunner in the 424th squadron.

After the War Bell returned to Canada and finally left the air force in 1961.

He remained in the aviation industry working for de Haviland and Spar Aerospace. Along with many of his old RCAF friends Bell retired in Trenton, Ontario, where Canada's largest and most active military airports is located.

In his later years he was able to use his vast knowledge and experience in aviation to help restore a Lancaster Bomber, which is exhibited at the Canadian Warplane Heritage Museum in his hometown of Hamilton. Gerry Bell died in 1989, aged 79.

The Lancaster Bomber was one of the most impressive planes of WWII. It was the only aircraft that could carry the 12,000lb Tallboy bomb and the 22,000lb Grand Slam bomb. Its wing span was 102ft and length was 69ft 6ins and was powered by four Rolls Royce or Packard Merlin engines. The Lancaster's most historic achievement was during the Battle of the Ruhr and the 'Dambusters' raid (see page 97).

Over 7,000 Lancasters were built during the war. Today only two are airworthy, and one of these was partly restored by Gerry Bell. This plane flew again for the first time on 24 September 1988.

Canada 107

PEOPLE PROFILE Sergeant Thomas George Prince MM SS

Canada's most decorated Aboriginal war hero

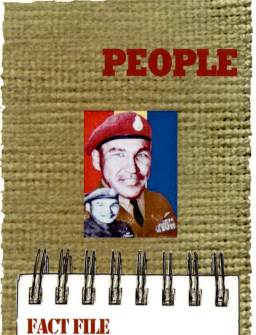

FACT FILE
D.O.B 15 October 1915
P.O.B Manitoba
D.O.D 25 November 1977
Tribe Ojibwa
Years of Service 193—1954
Rank Sergeant
Unit Royal Canadian Engineers
 1st Canadian Parachute Battalion
 1st Special Service Force Princess Patricia's Canadian Light Infantry (2PPCLI)
Engagements
 World War II
  France
  Italy
 Korean War
  Battle of Kapyong
Awards Military Medal (MM) (UK)
 Silver Star (USA)
 6 Service Medals for WWII
 4 Service Medals for Korea
Other Work
 Business owner
 Chairman of Manitoba Indian Association
 Lumberjack

Tommy Prince was born in a canvas tent. He was the great-great-grandson of the famous Chief Peguis, an 18th century Saulteaux chief.

Growing up on the Brokenhead reserve with his 10 brothers and sisters, 80 kilometres north of Winnipeg, he learnt from his father the hunting skills that were to become a key part of his life. In his teens, he joined the Army Cadets and honed his shooting skills; he could put five bullets through a target the size of a playing card at 100 metres.

At the start of the war, Prince volunteered and served with the Royal Canadian Engineers. In 1940 he volunteered for paratrooper service. The training was very difficult and Prince was one of just nine people out of 100 to graduate from parachute school in Manchester, England.

What distinguished him from the other trainees was his natural instinct for 'ground'. This meant that when he landed, he was able to crawl forward on his stomach with incredible speed and agility. He also knew instinctively how to conceal himself from view using small indents in an otherwise flat field; he was also a crack shot with a rifle.

By 1942 Prince returned to Canada and had been promoted to the rank of Sergeant in the 1st Canadian Parachute Battalion. His battalion merged with the United States Special Force, which was to become the elite 1st Special Service Force (see page 103). Prince was made a reconnaissance sergeant because of his unique hunting and field abilities.

On 8 February 1944, Sergeant Prince performed his most daring and dangerous feat in Anzio, Italy. His unit had been fighting for 90 days without relief on the frontlines. He went alone to an abandoned farmhouse in enemy territory and used it as an observation post. Prince ran a radio cable from the allied position to the farmhouse.

From here he was able to tell his colleagues the exact location of enemy troops so they could plan an attack. However, the communication line was suddenly cut. Immediately and without thinking of his safety, Prince found some farmer's clothes that had been left behind and changed into them. At the time, many Italian farmers had remained on their farms even though battles were taking place all around them.

Sergeant Prince then pretended to be an angry

"As soon as I put on my uniform I felt a better man."

Sergeant Prince was one of 59 Canadians awarded the US Silver Star and one of three awarded the Military Medal.

farmer; he went out into the field shaking his fists, shouting first at the enemy and then at the Allies. Then he went to work with a hoe in the field, in plain view of the enemy, when in reality, he was secretly following the radio cable and looking for the break. When he found it, he pretended to tie his shoelace, while secretly fastening the cable back together. He continued working in the field before going back to the farmhouse where he continued to transmit vital information to the Allies.

Once the enemy withdrew, Prince left his post and returned to his commanding officer.

For his outstanding bravery and daring, he was presented with a British Military Medal and an American Silver Star by King George VI at Buckingham Palace. After the War he returned to Canada and was honourably discharged from the armed forces in June 1945.

Prince's return to civilian life proved difficult at first. He was unable to find meaningful work where he could use his skills, so he worked as a lumberjack. However, as a veteran, he was able to get government assistance and set up his own successful cleaning business. In 1946 he was elected chairman of the Manitoba Indian Association. He lobbied the government for equal rights for his people, improved housing, and education and access to traditional lands.

In 1950 Prince returned to the Army to fight in the Korean War. He served on the frontline alongside Captain Reg Saunders and the Royal 3rd Australian Regiment (see page 18). Both Saunders' and Prince's regiments were awarded the United States Presidential Unit Citation for distinguished service in Kapyong.

Prince returned to Canada when War ended and was honourably discharged a year later in 1954 due to ill health. A combination of this, and his inability to use his wartime skills in civilian life meant he could only get menial jobs. He drank heavily, had little money and eventually separated from his wife and five children. Sadly, Sergeant Prince had to sell his prized medals to support himself.

He died in November 1977 at the age of 62. In 1997, after a nationwide fundraising campaign, Prince's family were able to buy back all of his medals at an auction for $75,000.

TRIBUTES

A street, a school, an army barracks and drill hall have been named after Prince.
He was also portrayed in the 1968 film "Devil's Brigade", as the character 'Chief'.

Project: For your eyes only

COVER STORY.
You are a journalist from the *Seagate Times* newspaper. You are helping the Prince family to raise money to buy back Sgt. Prince's medals.
Write an article in the newspaper about Sgt Prince's achievements to help the fundraising campaign.

Canada **109**

ACTIVITIES Games and Leisure

Games and leisure activities were very important to service personnel as they helped to boost morale. Sports also kept them physically fit and healthy.

Typical leisure and sports activities included:
- Music and singing
- Swimming
- Cricket
- Rugby
- Football
- Gambling
- Reading
- Card games

IWM H_037516

AWM 73521

TWO-UP
A traditional game from Australia

Two-up is a traditional Australian gambling game in which players gamble on whether two coins will fall with both heads up, both tails up, or with one coin falling as a head and one as a tail (known as Odds). It is traditionally played on ANZAC Day in pubs and clubs in Australia to commemorate the Diggers' wartime experience.

While it was illegal to play Two-Up, nobody minded when soldiers played during wartime. Since then it has been legalised and can be played on ANZAC Day in New South Wales. There are also several tourist 'Two Up Schools' in the Outback and it is offered as a table game in some casinos.

How to play
A person is selected as the Spinner; the rest of the players call them in by shouting "Come in, Spinner." The Spinner then tosses the coins in the air using the kip until the players win or lose.

AWM 025836

110

A wooden right-handed learner's kip.
AWM REL30802_007

The format of the game:
Two heads means the Spinner wins.
Two tails means the Spinner loses.
Odds means the Spinner throws again.

The Spinner is required to place a bet before the first throw which must be equalled by another later. If the Spinner wins he/she keeps both bets.
If the spinner loses, the money goes to the player who placed the bet. The Boxer takes a commission out of this bet.

The other players place bets against each other on whether the Spinner will win or lose.

Spinner The person who throws the coins up in the air. Each person in the group takes turns at being the spinner.
Boxer The person who manages the game and the betting, but doesn't participate in betting.
Ringkeeper (Ringy) The person who looks after the coins after each toss (to avoid loss or interference).
Kip A small piece of wood on which the coins are placed before being tossed.
One coin is placed heads up, the other tails up.
Heads Both coins land with the 'head' side facing up.
Tails Both coins land with the 'tails' side facing up.
Odds One coin lands with the 'head' side up, and the other lands with the 'tail' side up.

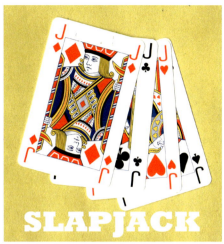

SLAPJACK

A fun card game which was played during the War

Objective: To win all of the cards.
Number of players: 2 to 8.

Deal one card at a time to each player, face down until all the cards have been dealt. It doesn't matter if players have different numbers of cards. Each players keep their cards face down and puts them into a neat pile in front of them.

The player to the dealer's left starts first by lifting the top card from their pile and dropping it face up in the middle of the table. The next player (to the left of the first player) does the same. Play continues in this way with each player putting their top card face up on the pile in the middle of the table.

If any player drops a Jack in the middle of the table, the first player to slap their hand on that Jack wins the entire pile of cards in the middle of the table. If more than one player slaps the Jack, the one whose hand is at the bottom wins the pile.

The winning cards must be put face down underneath the player's existing cards.

When a player loses all their cards they must watch for the next Jack and try to slap it, in order to win new cards. If they fail to slap the their hand on that Jack at this point and win the cards, then they are out of the game.

Play continues until one player has won all the cards.

Activities **111**

ACTIVITIES

Feeding the troops

During WWII, service men and women ate different foods depending on where they were stationed.

STATIONED AT A BASE
Food served would usually be the similar to that in civilian cafes, it was cooked in large amounts and soldiers had to eat quickly, so that the next group of soldiers could be served their share.

IN THE FIELD
If there was a field kitchen, soldiers were served by the unit's cooks who prepared food in large amounts. If there was no field kitchen then soldiers prepared their own rations.

IN COMBAT ACTION
Food was brought in through supply drops, usually in sacks and large tins. Sometimes it was not possible for the cooks to prepare hot food, in which case soldiers had to prepare their own food from their ration packs. Depending on their location, soldiers could also hunt animals for food, or ask friendly locals for bread and other basics.

LB02_8a

RATION PACKS
The contents varied depending on the nationality and religion of the soldier. For example Muslims and Jews do not eat pork and Hindus do not eat beef. However a typical ration pack could contain the following items:

- Hard biscuits – plain biscuits, ANZAC biscuits or rusks
- Dried meat or fish
- Tinned meat – such as corned beef (known as bully beef) or Spam
- Tinned fish – such as tuna or sardines
- Tinned goods – baked beans, stewed meats and vegetables and tomatoes
- Cereal biscuits – such as Weetabix or muesli bars, which could be eaten with or without milk, hot or cold
- Sweets – such as mints, chocolate, dried fruit or chewing gum
- Tea
- Coffee
- Powdered Milk
- Matches

Each ration pack would last for a specific period of time, for example 24 hours, and soldiers carried their rations in their packs. They also had to carry water bottles.

TASTY TREATS

ANZAC BISCUITS

ANZAC Biscuits are oatmeal biscuits whose main ingredients are rolled oats, coconuts and golden syrup.

They were originally made by Australian and New Zealand women for their loved ones who were fighting in World War I. The recipe, based on Scottish oatcakes, was created to ensure that the the biscuits would not break up and remained fresh as it would be many weeks before they reached the soldiers on the frontline.
There are no eggs to bind the mixture in ANZAC biscuits. This is because, during the War, many poultry farmers joined the services, so eggs were scarce. Instead golden syrup was used as a binding agent.

To this day ANZACS biscuits can still be found in Australian military ration packs. They also remain a popular snack food, sold in supermarkets as well as made in the home.

Ingredients:
1 cup plain flour
1 cup rolled oats
(regular oatmeal) uncooked
1 cup desiccated coconut
1 cup brown sugar
½ cup butter
2 tbsp golden syrup
1 tsp bicarbonate of soda
2 tbsp boiling water

Method:

Combine the flour (sifted), oats, coconut and sugar in a bowl.

Melt the butter and golden syrup in a saucepan over a low heat.

Mix the bicarbonate of soda with the water and add to the butter and golden syrup.

Pour the liquids into the dry ingredients and mix well.

Spoon dollops of mixture, about the size of a walnut shell, on to a greased tin leaving as much space between dollops to allow for spreading.

Bake in a moderate oven, 180C/350F for 15-20 minutes.

Cool on a wire rack and seal in airtight containers.

Enjoy!

BOBOTIE

Bobotie is a mildly curried meat dish which uses minced beef, pork or mutton cooked with spices in an egg custard. It originates from the Cape in South Africa where hundreds of years ago, it was a favourite recipe of the early Malay slaves.

Over the years it has become popular with all sectors of South Africa's diverse population and it is still a firm favourite today. It is usually served with yellow rice and sambals. but is also tasty served cold with a salad.

INGREDIENTS:
2 lbs (1Kilo) of minced meat
1 onion, chopped
1 thick slice of white bread, crusts removed
2 tablespoons apricot jam
2 tablespoons chutney
1 tablespoon oil
3 eggs, beaten
1 cup milk
2 tablespoons of lemon juice
2 teaspoons of curry powder
2 bay leaves (or lemon leaves)
salt to taste

METHOD:

Soak the bread in a cup of milk. Drain the milk and put to one side. Add the bread to the minced meat. Mix well with the jam, chutney, lemon juice, curry powder, and salt.

Heat the oil in a large pan. Add the onion and cook till soft. Add the meat mixture and brown, stirring all the time.

Put the mixture into a greased ovenproof dish.

Add the leftover milk to the eggs and beat together, then pour it over the meat mixture. Carefully place the bay leaves (or lemon leaves) on top and bake the bobotie in the oven at 350F/160C until the eggs are set. This should take about 45 minutes.

YELLOW RICE
2 cups uncooked rice
salt to taste
2 teaspoons turmeric
1 teaspoon sugar
1 cup seedless raisins (optional)
1 tablespoon butter (or margarine)
4 cups water

To cook the rice:
put all the ingredients, except the raisins, into a large pot and boil for 30 to 40 minutes. Add the raisins 5 minutes before the rice is cooked.

Serve the bobotie and rice with sliced banana and chutney.

Activities 113

ACTIVITIES: puzzles

International Morse code

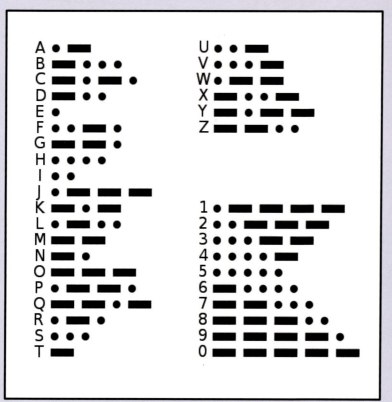

Starting on page 6, there is a Morse Code message shown on the grey panel at the bottom of each left-hand page. Using the key given here try to decode the message. Why not also try to convert your full name and address into Morse Code.

- A dash is equal to three dots
- The space between parts of the same letter is equal to one dot.
- The space between two letters is equal to three dots.
- The space between two words is equal to seven dots.

Word search puzzle

As we've learned, the countries listed below are just some of those which made up the British Empire. Can you find them in the wordsearch grid?

Words may read forwards, backwards, up, down, across or diagonally, but must always be in a straight line.

You may wish to use a pencil and eraser or photocopy the puzzle so that you don't mark the book permanently

```
L Q V L A L R K D I R H K P
U V M M Y F V A N J J H X X
L W A W A P V D B B R I G L
O E T C L F I L U B O K F N
H S O A A A P R S V O G E A
G T A M M O M F J B N W W I
A I R E N A Y C D M Z U J R
D N N R A X O P L E L R A E
A D C O H Y U G A N D A M G
N I J O L P N L V R O M A I
A E N N M Y A E Z V O F I N
C S B O R N E O K Q M R C N
L E Y W D J R C N F N M A D
A I L A R T S U A H C O E R
```

AUSTRALIA **JAMAICA**
BORNEO **KENYA**
BURMA **MALAYA**
CAMEROON **NEW ZEALAND**
CANADA **NIGERIA**
CEYLON **UGANDA**
FIJI **WEST INDIES**
INDIA

Answers are on page 120

Art and craft

Flanders poppy

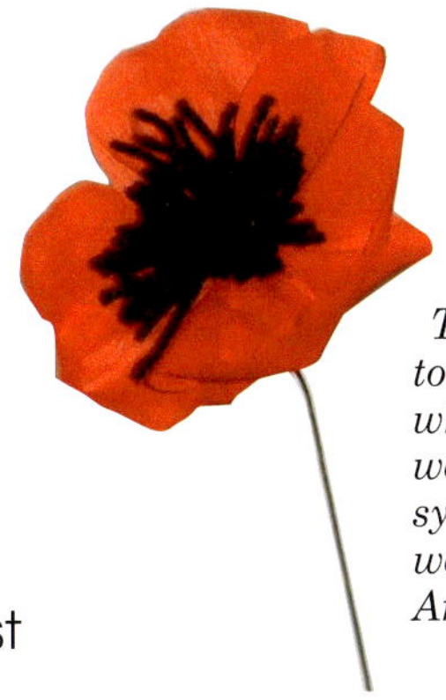

The Royal British Legion does its best to make sure that people remember those who have given their lives for the freedom we enjoy today. The poppy has become the symbol of remembrance worn during the weeks leading to Remembrance Sunday and Armistice Day.

You will need:
Red crepe paper approx 50cm wide and 10 cm long folded in four, (see diagram)
Black wool approx 3.5 m, scissors, 1 x 40mm length green stem wire (from garden or florist shops), masking tape, green poster paint

1 Fold the paper in half lengthways and then fold in half again
2 Cut four petal shapes as shown in diagram.
3 Stretch the centre of each petal gently by pulling it with your thumbs against the grain of the paper, then frill the top rounded edge by holding the sides of the petal in each hand and pulling it outwards between your thumbs and index fingers, taking care not to tear the paper.
4 Bend the top of the stem wire into a loop about 7cms from one end.
5 Make the black centre of the flower by winding the wool around your hand 20 times then tie it tightly in the middle with another piece of wool before cutting it through each end to make a pom-pom.
6 Thread the pom-pom through the loop and bend the wire down firmly to secure it tightly.
7 Position each petal carefully round the pom-pom by gathering the bottom edges round the stem. Tape them alltightly to the stem wire with masking tape.
9 Paint the masking tape green to match the stem.
10 Carefully ease the petals out and tease the black centre open.

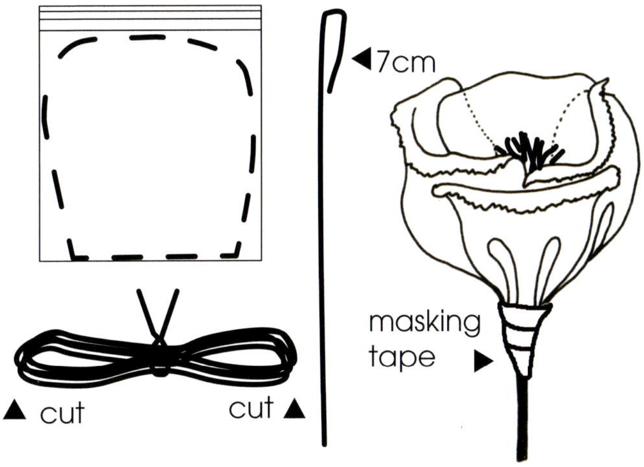

7cm
masking tape
cut
cut

Tribute card

Design a tribute card (like a citation) for some one you know who deserves to be recognised for something good or brave they have done,

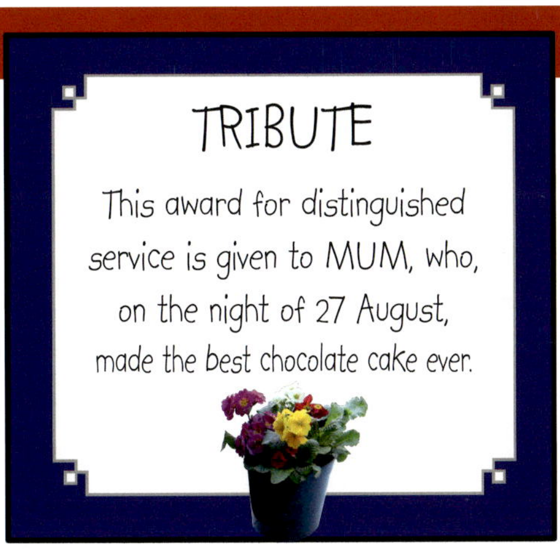

TRIBUTE
This award for distinguished service is given to MUM, who, on the night of 27 August, made the best chocolate cake ever.

You will need:
Coloured card
Coloured paper
Coloured pencils
Calligraphy pens
glue, scissors, ruler, poster paints, brushes
Transfer lettering (optional, available at most stationers and craft shops)
Magazines to cut up
Gift wrapping paper

Helpful hints:

Keep it simple. It is best to use strong, bold colours and cut shapes from coloured paper for the basic design

You could use a calligraphy pen to write the message, (there are usually books in the library which will give you guidance), otherwise use transfer lettering.

Look through magazines for interesting pictures that you can cut out and paste on to your card.

INDEX

1st Special Service Force 103, 108

14th Army 44, 55, 59, 75, 77

28th (Maori) Battalion 27, 28, 30, 31, 34, 35

28th (Maori) Battalion Marching Song 30, 31

81st (West Africa) Division 75, 76

82nd (West Africa) Division 75

Aboriginal(s) 14—21, 24, 25, 88, 100, 102, 108

Aboriginal flag 15

Abyssinia 10, 47, 59, 63, 72, 76, 80—83

Africa 11, 58, 59

African Auxiliary Pioneer Corps 68, 69, 70

Afrikaans 61

Algonquian 101

Anthony, Major Seth 76, 77

ANZAC 14, 15, 34, 110

ANZAC biscuits 23, 112

Army structure 13

Askari 81—83

Australia 11—22, 24 32, 36, 37

Australian Army 16, 18, 21

Australian Women's Army Service 24

Auxiliary Territorial Service 92

Bader, Leading Aircraftswoman Lilian 94

Baden-Powell, Lord 61

Bantu 60

Barbados 85, 91, 94

Basutoland 68

Battle of the Ruhr 96, 97, 107

Bechuanaland 68

Bell, Flying Officer Gerald (Gerry) 107

Beothuk 101

Biuku Gasa 36

Bletchely Park 82

Bobotie 113

Boer 17, 60, 61

Bombers for Britain campaign 90

Bose, Subhash Chandra 41, 51

British Cameroon (Cameroon) 59, 72, 73

British Commonwealth Air Training Plan 105

British Empire 8—10

British Empire Medal 70

British Guiana 88, 96

British Honduras 85, 90

British Honduras Forestry Unit 87

British Indian Army, Indian Army 42, 45, 47, 56

British Somaliland 11, 59, 81

British Southern Africa 68

British Togoland 72, 73

British West Africa 81

British West Indies (islands of) 85

Burma 41—43, 47—49, 54—59, 70, 72—73, 75—77, 82

Burma Rifles Scout 12

Burma Star 76, 77

Burma-Thai Railway 17, 55

Bushmen 60

Canada 94, 100—104, 106, 107

Canadian flag 101

Canadian Women's Army Corp 104

Cape Corps 62, 63

Ceylon 52

Changi 17, 53

Churchill, Winston 11, 33, 66, 86

Chevalier de la Légion d'Honneur 32

Chindit 11, 44, 55, 56, 59, 72, 82

Claude McKay 86

Coastwatchers 36, 37, 39

Colditz 51

Colony 8, 52, 59, 60, 72, 73, 80, 85, 100

Colour bar 102

Coloured Digger poem 25

Commonwealth of Nations 8

Conan Doyle, Sir Arthur 61

Conscription 10, 92, 102

Croix de Guerre 32, 50, 51

Cross, Squadron Leader Philip Ulric 98, 99

Dambusters 97, 107

Defence of Bathurst & Melville Islands 16

Devils Brigade 103

Diggers (Australian) 14, 15, 27, 110

Distinguished Conduct Medal 30, 66

Distinguished Flying Cross 48, 49, 98, 99

Distinguished Service Order 30, 98, 99

Dominion 8, 15, 101

Dutch War Commemorative Cross 20

East Africa 11, 41, 52, 58, 60, 61, 63, 70, 74, 80—83

East Africa Campaign 81, 83

Egypt 59, 63

Emperor Haile Selassie 80—83

Erinpura Voyage to Malta song 69

Eskimo 102

Ethiopia 59

Feeding the troops 112

Fiji 36, 38

Fiji Infantry Regiment 36—38

First Aid Nursing Yeomanry (FANY) 32, 50, 51, 92

First Nation 101, 102

Free French 72, 73

French Equatorial Africa 73

French Resistance 35, 50

French West Africa 72, 73

Gambia 72

Gandhi, Mahatma 40, 61

Geneva Convention 51, 55

George Cross Medal 13, 50, 51

George Medal 32, 33, 39

German East Africa 80

German U-Boat 89

Ghana 58, 59, 76, 77

Gideon Force 82, 83

Grant, Flight Lieutenant Cy 96

Gunditjmara 18, 19, 22

Gurkhas 41, 44, 45, 54, 57

Haka 28, 29

HRH Princess Elizabeth 92

HRH Prince Harry 5, 45

Hogan, Major Neville 56, 57

India 40—43, 45—51, 56, 57, 61, 81

Indian & Malay Corps 62, 63

Indian Armed Forces 43

Indian Maha Vir Chakra (MVC) medal 47

Indian National Army 41, 51, 52

Indian National Congress 41

Inuit 100—102

Italian East Africa 80

Jamaica 85, 90, 94

Johnson, Colonel Herbert 71

Johnson, Wallace 74

Keiha, Captain Kingi Areta 35

Kennedy, John F 36

Khan, Assistant Section Officer Noor Inayat 50, 51

Khoikhoi 60

Klootwijk, Hans 97

Kumana, Eroni 36

Lancaster Bomber 107

Lewis, Captain Neville 65—67

Lovett Family 22

Lynne, Dame Vera 57

Majozi, Lance Corporal Lucas 66, 67

Majumdar, Squadron leader Krishna 48, 49

Malaya 47, 48, 53

Maori 26—35

Manahi, Lance Sergeant Haane 31

Mandate 8

Martin, Brigadier Oliver M 106

Maseko, Lance Corporal Job 64, 65

Marshall, Albert 52

Mazumdar, Captain BN 51

Medal of Freedom 32

Member of the Order of the British Empire 18, 24, 30, 39, 56, 57, 70

Member of the Order of the Star of Ghana 76

Mentioned in Despatches 50, 70, 71, 76

Merchant Navy 52, 86, 88

Metis 102

Military and civilian equipment (donation of) 90

Military Cross Medal 30, 35

Military Medal 64, 65, 70, 108

Military ranks 13

Mobile canteens 91

Native Military Corps 62, 64, 66, 68

Negro 102

New Zealand 26—37

Ngarimu, 2nd Lieutenant Moana Nui a Kiwa 34

Ngata, Sir Apirana 27, 28

Nigeria 59, 72

Noonuccal, Oodgeroo 24, 25

North Africa 15, 41, 45, 47, 58, 60, 64, 66, 71, 74, 82

Northern Rhodesia 59, 68, 81

Northern Territory Special Reconnaissance Unit 16
Nyasaland 59, 68, 81
Order of Balboa 95
Order of Jamaica 95
Ossewabrandwag 62
Owens, Jesse 78
Pacific Islands 36, 37
Papua New Guinea (New Guinea) 18, 36, 38
Pearl Harbor 54
Prince, Sergeant Tommy 108, 109
Prisoner(s) of war (POWs) 17, 22, 51, 53, 55, 57, 63—65, 79, 87
***Quit India* campaign** 40
Protectorate 8
Red Cross 91, 102, 104
Rhodesia 59, 70
Rhodesian African Rifles 70
Royal Air Force 52, 59, 62, 73, 78, 82, 86, 94—99, 106
Royal Australian Air Force 16, 20, 21
Royal Australian Navy 16
Royal Canadian Air Force 102, 107
Royal Canadian Air Force Women's Division 105
Royal Canadian Engineers 108
Royal Indian Air Force/Indian Air Force 42
Royal Indian Navy, Indian Navy 43
Royal Navy 52, 61
Royal West African Frontier Force 12, 13, 74, 76, 77

Sanctuary 91
Saunders, Captain Reginald 18
Scrap metal 91
Selerang Barrack Square Incident 53
Shiftas 82
Sierra Leone 59, 72, 74, 78, 79
Sikh Regiment 46, 47
Singapore 11, 17, 45, 52—54
Singh, Jemadar Nand 46
Slave trade 59, 84
Slim, Field Marshal Sir William 44, 75, 77
Smythe, Flying Officer John Henry 78, 79
Smuts, Field Marshal Jan 61, 62, 82
Solomon Islands 36, 38, 39
South Africa 11, 59—69, 81, 83
South Pacific Scouts 37
Southern Rhodesia 11, 81
Special Operation Executive 32, 33, 50, 51, 83
St Lucia 89
Sukanaivalu, Corporal Sefanaia 38
Swazi Pioneers 71
Swaziland 68, 70, 71
Talalla, Flight Lieutenant Jimmy 53
Thompson, Flight Lieutenant Dudley 94, 95
Torres Strait Island flag 17
Torres Strait Island Light Infantry Battalion 16
Torres Strait Islanders 14, 16, 17

Trinidad 85, 92, 98
Trinidad Royal Naval Volunteer Reserve 88, 89
Two-Up 110, 111
Uniforms 12
US Legion of Merit 39
US Silver Star medal 39, 108
Vichy forces 72, 73
Victoria Cross medal 13, 27, 30, 34, 38, 41, 44—47, 60, 100
Viscount Slim 77
Vouza, Sir Jacob Charles 39
Wake, Captain Nancy 32, 33
Walker, Lance Corporal Kathleen 24, 25
Waters, Flight Sergeant Leonard 20, 21
Wavell, Field Marshal Sir Archibald 82
Weapons 12
West Africa 58, 61, 72, 73, 83
West African Campaign 73
West Indies 59, 84—94
Wingate, Major General Orde 82, 83
Women's Auxiliary Air Force 50, 94
Women's Auxiliary Australian Air Force 22, 23
Women's Auxiliary Corps (India) 43
Women's Royal Canadian Naval Service 105
Women's Royal Indian Naval Service 43
World War II Timeline 10

118

Acknowledgements

The author and publisher would like to thank the following organisations and people for their financial assistance to this project:

The Royal British Legion

Dr Moorad Choudry

The author would like to thank the following people for their kind assistance

- HRH Prince Harry
- LCpl Johnson Beharry VC
- Royal Commonwealth Ex-Services League
- Luke Billings
- Ziaur Rahman
- Emad Al-Ajlouni
- Margaret Beadman, AWM
- Cpl Garth O'Connell, Curator AWM
- Derek Robson, The RSL of Australia
- The guys from Seagate for rescuing my external hard drive
- Soroptimist International
- John Doble OBE
- Simon Tierney from the Far Setting Sun
- Grace Poulin
- Imperial War Museum
- Cy Grant
- Major Hogan
- LCpl Shaun Lovering (Royal Marines)
- Norm Peart
- Photographers:
  - Erick Myers
  - Emanuela Franchini
  - Cristina Cocullo
  - Danielle Deudney
  - Grant Deudney

Further Reading

War Bush: 81st (West African) Division in Burma 1943-1945
by John A. L. Hamilton (Michael Russell Publishing Ltd 2001)

Our War - How the British Commonwealth Fought the Second World War
by Christopher Somerville (Weidenfeld & Nicolson 1998)

A Member of the RAF of Indeterminate Race
by Cy Grant (WoodfieldPublishing 2007)

Invisible Women: WWII Aboriginal Servicewomen in Canada
by Grace Poulin (Thunder Bay 2007)

Colonies, Colonials and World War Two
www.bbc.co.uk/history/war by Marika Sherwood

Whose Freedom were Africans, Caribbeans and Indians Fighting for in World War II?'
Marika Sherwood with Martin Spafford (Savannah Press/BASA, 1999)

We served: the untold story of the West Indian contribution to World War II
by Angelina Osborne and Arthur Torrington (London: Krik Krak Publishing 2005)

The Black Diggers: Aborigines and Torres Strait Islanders in the Second World War
by Robert A. Hall (Allen and Unwin 1989)

Further Information

A Charmed Life: Jamaican veteran www.charmedlifecampaign.wordpress.com **Australian War Memorial** www.awm.gov.au
Bharat Rakshak, Indian Military Website www.bharat-rakshak.com
Canadian Warplane Heritage Museum www.warplane.com
Caribbean Aircrew www.caribbeanaircrew-ww2.com
Grace Poulin (author of Invisible Women) www.gracepoulin.com
Imperial War Museum www.iwm.org.uk
National Library of New Zealand www.natlib.govt.nz
Museum of Technology The Great War & WWII www.museumoftechnology.org.uk
National Army Museum (UK) www.national-army-museum.ac.uk
Royal British Legion www.britishlegion.org.uk
Royal Commonwealth Ex-Services League www.commonwealthveterans.org.uk
South African National Museum of Military History www.militarymuseum.co.za

Activities in the UK
Re-Enactment - become a Chindit!
Join or book the Far Setting Sun, Far East Living History Group, for a totally interactive and fun WWII experience with real uniforms and weapons. www.farsettingsun.co.uk

World War II Time Capsules
WWII Loan Boxes for Schools allow children to experience real objects and artefacts from the period in the classroom. Teachers' notes are provided. For more information contact the Museum of Technology The Great War & WWII on 01442 218381 or 01442 262541.

Photography credits

For permission to reproduce copyright pictorial material, the publisher gratefully acknowledges the following organisations and individuals:

Alexander Turnbull Library, New Zealand (ATL)
Australian War Memorial (AWM)
Imperial War Museum UK (IWM)
Koolshots/Canadian Warplane Heritage Museum (CWHM)
Kippenberger Military Archive, National Army Museum, New Zealand (KIP)
National Archives, UK (NA)
National Army Museum, UK (NAM)
Ministry of Defence UK (MoD)
Museum of Technology The Great War & WWII (MT)
South African National Museum of Military History and Delvillewood
This is England magazine (TIE)
US Library of Congress, Prints and Photographs Division
Flight Lieutenant Cy Grant
Danielle Deudney (DD)
Emanuela Franchini (EF)
Erick Myers (EM)
Grant Deudney (GD)
John Gibson, militaryfightingknives.com (JG)
Major Neville Hogan (NH)
Norman van Tasse, normsmedalmounting.com (NVT)

The image source (in brackets) and negative or reference number where applicable has been placed next to each image.

Every effort has been made to trace and acknowledge ownership of copyright. If any rights have been omitted, the publisher offers to rectify this in any future editions following notification.

Information included within is believed to be correct at the time of going to press. Neither the author nor the publisher can accept any responsibility for any error or subsequent change.

Answers to puzzles

The message given in code on the left hand pages throughut the book:

The Royal Commonwealth ex-Services League is a Charity which helps thousands of eligible veterans and widows who live outside the UK. During the war, help arrived from all corners of the globe. Now the people who helped Britain, at such a critical time, need our help. Many are now old and frail. The League provides vital financial and welfare assistance.

Credits and puzzle answers 120